EXPLORING
BLUE LIKE JAZZ

dixon kinser WITH donald miller

THOMAS NELSON
Since 1798

NASHVILLE   DALLAS   MEXICO CITY   RIO DE JANEIRO

Published in Nashville, Tennessee, by Thomas Nelson. Thomas Nelson is a registered trademark of Thomas Nelson, Inc.

Thomas Nelson, Inc., titles may be purchased in bulk for educational, business, fund-raising, or sales promotional use. For information, please e-mail SpecialMarkets@ ThomasNelson.com.

[Unless otherwise noted, Scripture quotations are taken from The Voice™, © 2012 by Ecclesia Bible Society. Used by permission. All rights reserved.]

ISBN: 9781418549534

Printed in the United States of America

12 13 14 15 16 QG 6 5 4 3 2 1

CONTENTS

FOREWORD

Many years ago I wrote the book Blue Like Jazz and I'm thankful. It was then and it is now a message in a bottle, a little letter thrown into the ocean in hopes there would be somebody whose story was similar. What I didn't know, and what I never expected, was to receive a million bottles containing similar letters in return. It seems we aren't alone at being alone, as the artist Sting has said.

And yet we go on believing, in some way, we are alone. We believe we are the only ones who struggle with unrequited love, with the desire to numb ourselves and check out. We believe we are the only ones who feel marginalized and unwanted, or who pine for sex, both appropriate sex and inappropriate sex.

One of the things that makes us feel most alone is when others do not acknowledge their own humanness. By humanness I'm talking about the reality of our condition, both beautiful and brutal. When others sit with us and pretend they are good, when truthfully they are both good and bad, we feel more alone in their company. This book is a book about not being alone.

Blue Like Jazz, as a movie, is about community. It's about a group of very diverse friends making their way through the world. It's a movie about the reality of life as it exists in transition, specifically the transition from high school to college. This transition is important because in our culture it's the time when people are leaving their previous selves and moving into a self of their own making. The transition to college is about making decisions, what to wear, what to drink, who to and whether to have sex, and what to believe.

This book is a book about making plans and having a strategy during that transition. I'm all for living in the moment, but reactionary living almost never works. Few teams win games by trying hard. They win games because they have a plan and they execute that plan. In this transition of our lives, the transition into finding ourselves, there are plenty of people who have a plan for you. The church has a plan for your soul, credit card companies have a plan your money, members of the opposite have a plan for your body. But what's your plan? And how will you know, when it comes time to make decisions whether or not their plan and your plan are the same? If you don't know, I promise, you'll be unknowingly stepping into their plan. And you'll never find yourself that way.

Take a group with you on this journey. Create a plan for yourself and walk with others as they create a plan for themselves.

—Donald Miller
Author of *Blue like Jazz*

INTRODUCTION

Growing Up Is Getting
Harder and Harder to Do

When I was a kid there was a country in Eastern Europe
called Yugoslavia. I knew Yugoslavia mainly for their comically bad
export—a sedan called the Yugo. But chances are you have never
heard of this country. That's because Yugoslavia doesn't exist
anymore. Sure, the space on the map where it used to be is still
there. It didn't get blown up or consumed by the earth or anything
like that. It's just that now what was once Yugoslavia has been
divided up into about a half dozen other nations. What used to
look one way on the map now looks very different—not because
the space on the globe has changed but because the boundary lines
have.

This is precisely what has happened in the past two decades
to the simple process of growing up. The timetable between
childhood and adulthood has shifted dramatically. Not because the
space on the map is different, but because boundary lines are. Ages
eighteen to thirty still exist. Though we haven't started to lose or
gain years on our lives, reaching full adulthood is a little trickier
than it's ever been. For some, this is cause for alarm. For others,
indifference. Personally, I find this hopeful. There are some very

specific reasons why all this is happening, but to understand them, we have to start where it all begins—adolescence.

Welcome to the Desert—You're Gonna Love It

Did you know that the concept of "adolescence" doesn't exist in most cultures and that it's only been around for about a hundred years in our own? For much of human history, the transition between childhood and adulthood was swift and abrupt and had a steep learning curve. One day you were a kid in your parents' home with fairly domestic responsibilities, and the next you were married or working in a factory—or both. However, significant social changes around the turn of the twentieth century (like the introduction of child labor laws, universal schooling mandates, and the advent of public education) created a gap between the onset of puberty and full adult autonomy. Suddenly there was this prolonged dependence between children and their families where so-called teenagers could develop psychologically outside of the pressure of survival and manual labor. This space gave birth to a new stage of life called adolescence.[1] Psychologist Stanley Hall is largely credited with "discovering" adolesence in 1904, but he really didn't "discover" anything. Hall simply *observed* a developmental phenomenon that was happening right under everyone's noses, and a hundred years later, it's happening again.

Our culture uses four benchmarks to indicate the end of adolescence and the beginning of full adulthood:[2] the end of schooling, a stable job, financial independence, and the formation of a new family.[3] A century ago, these were each able to meet much earlier in life. However, by the end of the twentieth century, the finish line of full adulthood seemed to be moving further and further away. The stable jobs of two generations ago, once readily available with a high school diploma or bachelor's degree (think factory work, manufacturing, and entry-level business positions), started to disappear or move overseas. At the same time, other career tracks started requiring more and more specialized training (think graduate and postgraduate degrees) to even get your foot in the door. This meant at least three benchmarks of full adulthood —the end of education, a stable job, and financial independence—weren't even possible until one's mid-twenties or early thirties. As a result, the last marker of full adulthood—new family formation—ends up on the farthest back burner—if it was even being considered at all. Does this sound familiar? This new mix of economic, social, and cultural factors have all worked together to open up another developmental gap in the young adult experience. It's name? Emerging adulthood.[4]

That's right, like adolescence a century ago, emerging adulthood is a new developmental concept. It describes the phase of life between the end of adolescence (circa eighteen years old) and the beginning of full adulthood (circa thirty years old), and includes more than forty million people in the United States alone.[5] However, like each of the "phases of life" that have come before it, emerging adulthood is the result of many factors (biological, cultural, institutional, and economic). Therefore, the duration of this will be a different experience for everyone. And there's the rub.

Growing up is harder than it used to be.

Because emerging adulthood is new space on the human developmental map, there are no well-worn trails or tried-and-true strategies to get through it. Not anymore. This causes many emerging adults (EAs) a certain amount of anxiety. I hear it all the time from the young people I work with, and it comes out in sentiments like, "I just really thought I'd have *fill in the blank* by the time I was twenty-five" or, "I always thought I'd be married by *this age*." And when you think about it, their incredulity is understandable because, for most people, there is a pretty predictable formula for how life will unfold through adolescence. You go to middle school and practice getting good grades so that when you're in high school (and grades start counting) you have developed the right kind of study habits so you can take the right number of AP classes and get the best marks so that those grades, when coupled with your extracurricular activities, will position you to get into a superior college, that you will attend with the scholarship money you've earned, and then after you graduate you'll . . . well, uh, now it starts getting kind of fuzzy. What happens next? What's *supposed* to happen next? No one knows. Or to be more precise, everyone knows but no one is sure how to get there.

It's like this part of life is a big triathlon, except that the middle leg is now an episode of *The Amazing Race*. In *The Amazing Race*, teams compete to reach checkpoints all over the globe, and the challenge is that they are totally on their own in choosing how they get to each one. They can take a plane, swim a river, or take a taxi, and each team alone bears the consequences of any wrong turns they make. Choose well and you'll be in first place. Choose poorly and you may not make it at all.

So, imagine you start the triathlon in adolescence running a fairly predictable course (middle school to high school to college, and so on.) Then you reach the end and all you see is a vast desert. Suddenly, the host of *The Amazing Race*, Phil Keoghan, hands you an envelope and says, "There's a checkpoint on the other side of this desert that you can't see from here but you're on your own as to how you get there. There are no roads or landmarks in this desert and very few people have done this yet, so do your best. See you on the other side!" How would you feel facing such a challenge? Intimidated? Exhilarated? Resentful? Hopeless? I think there is a little of each of these in the emerging adult experience. Life made so much sense for so long and now there's just a big desert.

Everything was so regimented and predictable through high school, and now it's just . . . this. How am I supposed to make it across? That's where a book like this comes in.

Exploring Blue Like Jazz is a book about how to do life and faith well during emerging adulthood. It's a book intended to make "growing up" a little easier. Donald Miller and I put it together because there are so few resources out there for people crossing this big, big desert and we wanted to offer one. However, there is nothing quick and easy about our approach. What we hope to do is offer EAs (and their communities) some tools for making a life that flourishes and glorifies God during this peculiar phase of development.

I'm connecting this book to the movie adaptation of *Blue Like Jazz* because the whole film works like a big object-lesson for the kinds of conversations, issues, and struggles EAs are having in our day.[6] I'll reference the film every now and then to provide a point of continuity between the movie and the book; however, you do not have to have seen *Blue Like Jazz* to use this book as a valuable resource. This book is less of a "movie-based study guide" and more of a "field manual for EA Christian living." The book contains discussion questions to help you start helpful conversations, as well as journaling opportunities for individuals and groups. Use them. This time of life, like any other, is not to be traveled alone or without intention. I hope the discussion guides in each section will inspire you to find some traveling companions (if you don't have them already). All of which brings me back to the desert.

If emerging adulthood is a kind of desert, remember, God's people have experienced the desert in two ways. It has been both a place of struggle, pruning, and discipline (I'm thinking here of the Israelites wandering, David's hiding, and Jesus' temptation), as well as a place of refreshment and renewal (as it was for fathers and mothers of the early church who went to the desert because it was the best place for their faith to grow). What about for you? How are you experiencing emerging adulthood so far? Is it a place of struggle or of renewal? Perhaps a bit of both? Either way, remember that Christians have flourished in the desert for centuries and so

can

you.

How to Read the Rest of This Book

This book is like a toolbox for emerging adults, along with their parents, friends, and mentors, to use while working out what faithfulness to God means during emerging adulthood. From this point forward, it does not have to be read straight through like a novel, but can be accessed topically like Wikipedia. The following pages contain guides to eleven topics germane to emerging adulthood and teed up by the movie *Blue Like Jazz*. There is also an appendix with a five-week curriculum based on each of the five "precepts" of life we lay out in the back of the book for use with small groups, youth groups, or Bible studies. Our prayer is that you and your community will engage the content of the book and its movie to grow together as Christians emerging into adulthood and glorifying God in the process.

CHAPTER 1

ALCOHOL

I vividly remember the day I turned sixteen years old, because I was finally able to go to the DMV to get my driver's license. I was excited and nervous. What if my training in Driver's Ed wasn't sufficient? What if I couldn't remember how to execute the three-point turn? What if I forgot the answers to the written test?

Despite my hand wringing, I passed (not with flying colors, but I passed) and later that afternoon sat behind the wheel of a car for the first time by myself. Instead of feeling elated at the possibility of freedom, I panicked. *Oh my goodness! I remember thinking. Can I really do this? I could kill somebody in this thing. Are they sure I'm capable of this? Because I'm not sure that I am.* It took me about ten minutes to calm down enough to start the car and actually get on the road. I'm not sure the perspective I had in that moment always stayed with me as a teenage driver, but I've thought back to that afternoon many times over the years. It was a rare moment (and I've had a few of them since) when I was aware of the seriousness of the situation I was in just before I entered it. I knew that the fact that I could now drive was a big deal and, at the risk of sounding sanctimonious, the responsibility to handle it well was uniquely my own.

I wonder if our relationship to alcohol works the same way. There is a responsibility to handle drinking well that belongs to each of us, individually. We learn lots of things about drinking from multiple sources (parents, teachers, preachers, TV shows, and movies, to name a few), and we form our opinions by integrating those individual messages into our own unique belief. However, the actual choices we make about alcohol belong to us alone. So, the question is, "How do I make good choices?" What do you think healthy and life-giving choices in regard to alcohol look like? How can you tell the difference between alcohol use that is helpful and that which is hurtful? And, most importantly, do we drink to the glory of God? These are some of the questions this chapter attempts to answer.

So, as we get going, remember that picture of a sixteen-year-old sitting behind the wheel of his parents' car. Like driving, drinking is something we should respect because, if we're careless, things can go really wrong. However, with a little training and a few boundaries, they don't have to. Moderation is not something that is self-evident. It takes some forethought and intentionality. So allow me to put some things on the table that will keep us "on the road" as it were, so that when (and if) we drink alcohol, we can do it in the name of Jesus.[1]

Our Take...
Alcohol Doesn't Make Bad Decisions.
People Do.

I was on vacation last summer and a car passed me on the highway with a bumper sticker that said "Guns don't kill people. I do." As terrifying a notion this is, the point seems to be that it's not the guns that are dangerous, but instead the people who use them. This is actually a helpful distinction when applied to our choices about alcohol.

Alcohol is not something that is inherently bad or evil on its own. Sometimes Christians react to alcohol's misuse by decreeing that all alcohol should be off limits. But this turns it into some sort of cursed talisman that corrupts the user (like Frodo and the One Ring), which I think is a little extreme. The responsibility for alcohol's misuse needs to go where it actually belongs, and that is with the drinker. This is why the Scriptures don't condemn drinking alcohol. In the Bible, alcohol is part of the life of God's people and is even included in one of Judaism's most sacred rituals.[2] What the Scriptures do condemn, however, is drunkenness.[3] Getting drunk is not part of God's right-side-up world. It's not part of the kingdom. However, just because alcohol can be misused doesn't mean the drink itself is bad. Alcohol doesn't make bad decisions . . . people do.

I don't want to minimize the reality that when alcohol is overused things can go extremely wrong. Drunkenness and high-risk behavior seem to go hand in hand. There are tragic statistics about its role in sexual assault among emerging adults. One in four women will be sexually assaulted during their four years on a college campus. One in four! And in 95 percent of the cases, it will be by someone the victim knows. About half of these reported sexual-assault cases involved alcohol usage by the perpetrator, the victim, or both.[4]

But it doesn't stop there. Even though drunk driving is known to be dangerous, a 2000 CDC study found that almost 40 percent of college-aged participants' admitted to riding with a drunk driver within one month of the study. Even though the danger is obvious, these emerging adults did it anyway. This kind of high-risk behavior may be why alcohol-related fatalities continue to rise among emerging adults, up 3 percent since 2003.[5] All told, alcohol misuse contributes to 1,825 student deaths, 599,000 injuries, and 97,000 cases of sexual assault or date rape each year.[6]

These statistics are nothing to take lightly, because they are realities you will likely encounter. Alcohol is a player in some of the worst violence and sexual degradation that happens between emerging adults, but it still doesn't make alcohol itself bad. You can start to change things by making good choices. Christians interested in being part of the solution to all this, rather than part of the problem, need to make a game plan for how, when, why, and with whom they are going to drink. Ad hoc choices involving alcohol are not good enough. Drinking in a way that loves both God and neighbor needs some careful preparation, and it is to this task we now turn.

Planning on Drinking?

Have you ever seen those bumpers they put up on the lanes in the bowling alley? The bumpers help kids learn to bowl by giving their ball some boundaries to bounce off of while it travels down the lane toward the pins. The bumpers don't control the path of the ball; they just keep it out of the gutter. Below are four guidelines meant to serve as bumpers on the bowling alley of your choices with alcohol. They are not here to control you; rather they represent the collection of accumulated wisdom that will help you be part of the solution with your drinking, and not part of the problem.

1. If You're Underage, Don't Drink.

This may go without saying, but if you are not of legal age, please do not drink alcohol.[7] As I mention in the chapter on partying, I do not disagree with the fact that it may be unfair that you can vote, fight in a war, and drive a car before you can have a drink in the United States. However, your right to have a glass of wine before you are twenty-one is not a justice issue. While there are indeed places Christians are called to break the law for the sake of the gospel, this is not one of them.[8] If you're not yet of age, just hang back and don't drink. Self-control is one of the fruits of the Holy Spirit. You can handle this.[9]

2. Don't Get Drunk.

If no one has ever said this to you, then let me be the first. Don't get drunk. It is simply not good for our bodies and doesn't tend to bring about goodness in either the life of the drinker or those around them. This is not a Christian-fascist attempt to control your life but a sober (pardon the pun) admission that, as the statistics imply, bad things can happen when people drink too much. Choosing moderation keeps you and everyone around you safe while you're drinking. I'm pretty sure most people involved in criminal and violent behavior while under the influence don't set out to assault someone before they have their first cocktail. However, the perception of right and wrong can change as people start to lose control. Drinking alcohol is fine, but doing it to get drunk is not.

Strategically, this just means knowing both your limits and your family history. How many drinks can you have and not get drunk? Ever tested it out? Try keeping a drinking journal for a month. Use it to chart how many drinks you have, what kind of drinks you have, and how often you drink every week. A journal like this can give you a good idea of when to say when. If you have no idea where to start, try this: Most men are recommended to have no more than two drinks a day and fourteen per week. For women (and men over the age of sixty-five) it drops to one drink a day and seven per week.[10] Shoot for these boundaries and see how you fare. Figuring out your limits is the first step toward healthy alcohol use.

However, your limits should be influenced by your family's history with alcohol. While there are no definitive studies that prove alcoholism is passed down from parent to child, children of alcoholic parents can be at a greater risk of alcohol dependency than others. This may be genetic or simply come from a distorted perspective of alcohol use. Either way, if you have alcoholism in your family, seek the counsel of a therapist or mentor before you begin drinking. This will minimize your risk and help you develop healthy limits.[11]

3. Drink with People You Know in Familiar Places

With the aforementioned statistics on sexual assault in mind, if you're going to drink, know with whom you are drinking. Alcohol lowers inhibitions and can make you prone to poor decisions. So, even if he's really cute and very charming at the party or she's really sweet and funny at the bar, going to an unfamiliar place with an unfamiliar person after you've been drinking is a bad idea. It can put both of you at risk, especially if one of you has had too much to drink. If you don't know someone well and you're going to meet them for a drink, get together in public and stay within your limits. If you want to go somewhere private with that person, consider not drinking beforehand. It's easy to have fun without alcohol and if the person you're hanging out with can't respect your choice not to drink, they may not be worth hanging around with after all.

Similar to knowing *who* you are drinking with, you should also know *where* you are drinking. Drinking in an unfamiliar place can be super risky when it comes time to leave. My friends who work on university campuses recommend not drinking anywhere you can't walk home from in thirty minutes. Would that work for you? Where are the places within thirty minutes of your home that you could meet others for a drink? Who can you walk with in order to stay safe? What parameters would you need to have in place if you want to drink in a place that is unfamiliar? Make a plan ahead of time and you'll have no problem making healthy decisions that keep you, and others, out of harm's way.

4. Get Relational about Your Drinking

I was talking to a friend about drinking recently, and he admitted to me that when he drinks too much it's because he wants the alcohol to help him get closer to people. He told me, "When I wanted to feel close to the people I was around, I drank with them. The more I drank, the closer I felt to those around me. As it turns out, just the opposite was true. The more I drank, the more my behavior damaged the relationships I was trying to build.

I had to start evaluating my drinking based on how it affected my relationships. That's when things started to make sense."

What my friend was picking up on is that drinking right, like most of the choices Christians make in life, involves more than just following rules. Good choices can best be made when they are evaluated through the lens of how they affect our relationships. This is what I mean . . .

In the beginning when God creates the heavens and the earth, all of the relationships in the creation are whole, healthy, and integrated.[12] The two human beings are naked and feel no shame (their relationship to self is intact), they compliment and need each other (their relationship to others is whole), they live in the garden (their relationship to the creation is undamaged), and they both work with God to cultivate it (their relationship with God is unbroken).

But you know what happens next.

The human beings rebel, sin and death enter the creation, and everything that God made right-side up is turned upside down. Their relationship with God is broken (when God shows up, they hide[13]). The relationship they have to themselves is broken (they are ashamed of their nakedness[14]). Their relationship to one another is broken (when God asks what happened, they blame each other[15]). And finally, their relationship to the creation itself is broken (they have to leave the garden[16]). However, God doesn't give up. He mounts a rescue mission to put everything that was broken back together, to heal the fractured creation and make things as they were meant to be.[17] Jesus accomplishes this act in His death and resurrection, and people like you and I are left to implement it. We do this good work anytime we bring to restoration one or more of the four broken relationships.

Are you still with me?

All of this gives us a framework to help us evaluate our moral choices, beyond just rules.[18] Paying attention to these four vital relationships can help us make healthy and responsible choices regarding alcohol. Jesus' gospel is not about the imposition of new rules for His followers anyway. It is about a life of freedom and hope that embodies the fact that God is actually putting everything back together. So, when you approach alcohol, begin by asking, "Are my choices moving toward some kind of healing and wholeness in each of these four relationships or not? Am I moving toward restoration with this choice or back toward brokenness?" Then think about who you can ask to help you figure out if you are doing it right. Evaluating our choices in this way makes space for us to enjoy one of God's good gifts: alcohol.

This Is My Blood...

One last thought to close things out.

My son started taking communion at our church when he was about seven years old. Because we use very sweet wine in my parish (a port to be precise) and he is into anything with sugar in it, it wasn't long before the wine was his favorite part of worship. One night during our family dinner, my wife and I were having wine. My son turned to me and said, "Can I have a sip of that?" "No," I responded, "we're not in worship, we're at dinner. Drinking wine here is different than during Communion." ("Besides this is a Cabernet and you wouldn't like it anyway.") In thinking about my gut response, I have to wonder if perhaps I was wrong. Not about a seven-year-old drinking table wine, but that drinking alcohol in worship is somehow different than drinking alcohol everywhere else.

For thousands of years, many Christians have celebrated the Lord's Supper with alcohol. It's one of the central symbols in the rite. The cup of wine in the Christian Eucharist actually comes from the three of four cups of wine consumed during the Jewish Passover meal. Each of those cups of wine has a special, symbolic significance relating to God's promises of freedom to His people.[19] The one that Jesus made "His blood" that night is called the cup of Redemption; it is preceded by the cup of Sanctification and Deliverance and then followed by the cup of Praise.

Sanctification, redemption, deliverance, and praise are all remembered and enacted by the drinking of a cup of wine.

Christians take up the symbolism of the four cups in their Eucharistic celebrations. But what if that's not the only place we are meant to take them up? What if every time we drink alcohol, it is an opportunity to remember and enact the promises of the four cups? What if God's promises of freedom could be on display every time Christians drank alcohol? What if that's how it's supposed to be? Would that give us new eyes to see how, when, where, and why we are drinking? Would it help us see how God might be inviting us to join His healing of the world? And might it also challenge us to drink alcohol in a way that looks forward to that great moment when we drink the last cup with Jesus in the Messianic kingdom?[20]

When Jesus offered the cup of Redemption to His disciples, He gave them a cup of alcohol. His first followers shared that cup remembering His words to them, "This cup is the new covenant, executed in My blood. Keep doing this, and whenever you drink it, you and all who come after will have a vivid reminder of Me."[21]

May you seek redemption in everything you do with alcohol. May the Holy Spirit empower you to make healthy and safe choices in the way you drink, and may He grant you the strength to abstain from alcohol if you choose to do so. If and when you choose to drink, be sure to do it for the remembrance of Him.

THE WAY IN

Watch a TV commercial for alcohol online as well as Don's DVD clip on alcohol.

1. How is the company selling their product? Are they selling alcohol as the best way to achieve a cool image?[22]

2. How do you see alcohol consumed around you?

3. When you hear the word *moderation*, what do you think of?

4. How is alcohol use generally portrayed on TV and in the movies? Where have you seen accurate portrayals of it, and where have you seen it portrayed inaccurately?

EXPLORING FURTHER

1. Do you drink alcohol? Why or why not?

2. Have you ever been tempted to drink too much? What were the circumstances?

3. Do you believe the author's four-relationship ethic is a helpful one for making choices about drinking?

4. What other circumstances could the four-relationship ethic be applied to?

5. Is there ever a time Christians should not drink? If so, when?

6. Is there ever a time Christians should drink? If so, when?

CRAFTING YOUR RULE

1. Make a drinking journal. List Monday through Sunday and mark every day you've had a drink, what you drank, and what time of day it was.

2. How often do you drink alcohol? Where are you when you drink?

3. If you gave up drinking for a month (say you gave it up for Lent), would that be hard or easy? Why?

4. What will be the most difficult thing about making a plan for how you use alcohol?

5. Who would join you in creating a drinking journal, or in drinking more responsibly?

6. What are you most afraid of as you move forward?

7. What is your strategy for dealing with that fear in a healthy way? Who will you talk about it with? What will your life look like without that fear?

CHAPTER 2

CONFESSION

For my day job, I am an Episcopal priest and I love what I do. However, I have one of the few jobs that when you tell people what you do for a living, they immediately start apologizing. For example, if they've used profanity anywhere in our conversation, as soon as they find out I'm a priest they'll say, "Oh, sorry about my cussing." Or if I saw them smoking, they'll apologize for it and explain that they are trying to quit. These are funny examples, but there are more serious ones as well. I have had numerous colleagues tell me stories about taking airplane trips wearing their clergy collars only to have the stranger sitting next to them break down and spend the whole flight unloading years of personal pain. What does it mean that people will share the worst of what has happened to them with a total stranger on an airplane? I wonder if it demonstrates the way people are really looking to get their "stuff" out but don't have a place to do it. They want to talk about the burdens they are carrying around, but because they don't have a way to do it, it gets pent up and pushed down until they're on a red-eye sitting next to a priest. We all carry around pain from the wrongs that have been done to us. Dealing with those wrongs is called choosing forgiveness. But we also carry around the burden of the wrongs we have done to others, and dealing with those wrongs is called *confession*, which involves asking for forgiveness.

Our Take...

One of the most powerful scenes in the movie *Blue Like Jazz* involves confession. At the end of Renn Fayre, all the students line up to confess their sins to "the pope" of Reed college. Don, who has just been consecrated pope, has an epiphany before he hears his first confession. He realizes that before he can hear anyone else's confession, he needs to ask for forgiveness for the ways he has misrepresented God. Don's expression of candor and vulnerability actually opens up a space for healing the life of the former "pope" and is one of the more beautiful moments in the film.

When I first encountered this story, I loved how it seemed to turn the dynamic of confession on its head. Like most people, I thought of confession simply as a personal declaration of wrongdoing. But that's only half of it. Confession also involves listening. In *Blue Like Jazz*, it's the fact that there is someone in that booth *hearing* the confession that makes the healing possible. This is because confession includes both a speaking component and a listening component. When these two occur together, it makes space for God to repair our hearts.

Speaking Confession

I was twenty-two the first time I ever did a formal confession. Since I did not grow up in a church tradition that encouraged frequent or even regular confession, I was unfamiliar with what I was supposed to do and pretty nervous about doing it. The occasion for my confession was a class I was taking in graduate school. It was about Christian spiritual formation, and one of the homework assignments was to make a sacramental confession. This meant we had to go to an authorized church leader (in my case, a priest, because I was Episcopalian) and actually, personally, *out loud*, confess our sins and receive forgiveness.

I was doing youth ministry at the time so I asked the priest I worked for to hear mine. Because he was a friend, I felt confident it would make things easier and less awkward. I was so wrong. On the afternoon we met to do this, I was a nervous wreck. He had given me a worksheet to help me think through what I might confess during our time together, but as I looked over what I had written down, I started to get cold feet. Was I really going to admit these things to him? What would he think of me afterward? What if he thinks less of or is ashamed of me? I know how judgmental I am—will he be the same? Silencing these voices as best I could, I walked into the church and down to his office more unsure than ever that this was a good idea.

We opened the Book of Common Prayer to begin (that's the place where the Episcopal Church has a liturgy to guide this process) and I got some of the best advice I have ever received regarding confession. He told me that when it comes to speaking my confession, it was best to be as truthful, detailed, and specific as I could be. This, he explained to me, was because when our wrongs are spoken aloud, they are brought out into the open. This kind of exposure breaks the shame and power these sins have over us because when we bring things into the light, he continued, we don't have to be afraid of them anymore.

Is it strange to say that confession reminds me of the movie *Jaws*? I promise you, the metaphor isn't as crazy as it sounds! *Jaws* was Steven Spielberg's first big hit movie, but the production was famously problematic. The movie's villain is a great white shark, and because you can't exactly train a shark to play a part in a movie, Spielberg had to improvise. He had a mechanical shark constructed to play the menacing role, but it kept malfunctioning. As a result, Spielberg couldn't shoot as many scenes with the shark as he wanted to and was forced to keep glimpses of the shark to a minimum. This meant that the director could only hint at the monster's presence and had to save any full views of the shark for the last reel and the final confrontation with the film's protagonist. The result is a masterpiece of suspenseful storytelling that worked better than the director himself could have hoped. What you don't see of the monster is what makes it so threatening. *Jaws* demonstrates an all-important lesson: once you see something in the light and its edges are revealed, it's just not as scary anymore.

Speaking our confessions works the same way. It is fear that makes us apprehensive to share our failings and speak honestly about our shortcomings. We are afraid of judgment, afraid of being the only one who struggles with a certain issue, afraid that what lurks on the inside of us is so big and bad it will overtake us if we speak it out loud. But nothing could be further from the truth. Proverbs 28:13 says it this way: "Whoever tries to hide his sins will not succeed, but the one who confesses his sins and leaves them behind will find mercy."

The power our sins have over us come from their concealment. It is their concealment that keeps giving them the upper hand, which is why there's a saying in twelve-step recovery groups that you are only as sick as your secrets. When we speak our confession aloud so others can hear it, our pain becomes like that shark in *Jaws*—no longer scary because in the light, we can see the edges.

Hearing Confession

When I finished confessing my sins against God and my neighbor, my friend gave me some counsel for holy living, and then he reminded me that God had forgiven my sins as I had confessed through something our tradition calls an absolution. I felt like a different person. He was right. Getting it all out really changed me. I wasn't afraid anymore. I mean, to be that vulnerable in front of someone and have them respond with forgiveness, restoration, and acceptance was really incredible. I had been given this gift, and the most natural response seemed to be to say thank you—to God for His mercy and forgiveness, and to my friend for listening. The restoration and new life I experienced really did take more than just speaking; somehow it required someone else to do some listening as well.

James 5:16 has this admonition: "So own up to your sins to one another and pray for one another. In the end, you may be healed." I love the way this text connects confession and healing. They really do go together. When we confess our sins, we are driving them out of us, but God doesn't leave an empty void behind where our since once were. With the space that is left, God can move in and heal us. Heal us from our patterns of doing this thing over and over again. Heal us from our bitterness. Heal us from our jealousy of others who we think have it better than us. God's mission in this world is one of healing and restoration, so it makes sense that God might do the same thing with us. When we confess our sins *to* another person, it opens up a door for healing to take place.

But the key element in the James text is that the confession that leads to healing happens from one person to another. If you're going to confess in a way that heals, there needs to be another person there to hear it. Hearing confession makes healing possible just as much as speaking does. They work together. I wonder if the reason people melt down confessing to strangers on airplanes is not because we lack the skill to speak our confession as much as we lack the people who will listen. Is this part of the reason we feel so overwhelmed by trauma, trapped in addictions, and exhausted by our guilt—because we have no space in our relationships to listen to one another? And if we have no clear place for someone to listen to the wrongs we have done and the wrongs that have been done to us, we might get so desperate we will unload on a total stranger—even someone wearing clericals sitting in coach.

What do you think it would take to change that? What can you do to be someone who hears people's stories and provides healing? Is there anyone who already comes to you to share their pain? What would it look like for you to confess your sins and pray for someone so that they might be healed?

"For Y'all Have Sinned and Fallen Short of the Glory of God..."

The last thing I want to say about confession is it may start as a personal activity but it doesn't end there. Confession has a communal dimension to it, because sin is something communities can be complicit in as much as individuals. People create cultures, systems, and institutions to direct and shape our common life.

When we do this, our capacity for bending away from God does not magically disappear. On the contrary, it remains well intact and because of this, our communal lives together can either reflect God's good character or rebel against it. You've probably seen this firsthand already. It can be a family that cultivates a self-centered spirit, turning a blind eye to those around them in need. Or it can be a group at work or school that consistently brings negativity and complaints out of everyone who comes into their orbit. These are sins that not just one person commits but groups of people do. They are sins of commission and omission. For these things, we must also openly, actually, and audibly repent.[1]

There is much more to be said on this topic than I have room to say here, but because confession in the Scriptures is most often a communal thing,[2] we need to remember that personal confession is just the tip of the iceberg. Confessing sin can be a path to healing not just for individuals but also for whole cultures and cities as well. Because God's desire is for the healing and restoration of the world, let us explore how our communal speaking and hearing of each other's confession can join God in making that happen.

THE WAY IN . . .

Watch the section of the movie when Don is in the confession booth at Renn Fayre, followed by the DVD clip on confession.

1. Why do you think all those students are lining up? Are they taking this seriously? Why did you answer the way you did?

2. How is Don's confession to the pope a healing moment? Who gets healed?

3. What do you think about the office of "pope" at Reed College in the movie? Do you think it shows a respect of God or not?

Watch the scene at the beginning of the movie where Don's youth pastor teaches James 5:16 during the lock-in and Don questions him about it.

4. Do you think there is a connection between forgiveness and healing? What is it?

5. Do you have anything you want to be healed of? What do you do with that desire?

EXPLORING FURTHER . . .

1. What's the most threatening thing to you about the prospect of confession?

2. Have you ever gone to a priest or religious leader to make a sacramental confession? What was it like?

3. Is it harder to "speak" a confession or to "hear" one?

4. Do you agree with the author's statement that sin can be communal as well as individual? Why or why not?

5. Where do you think your current community is sinning?

6. How can your confession contribute to the whole creation's healing?

CRAFTING YOUR RULE

1. What do your friendships look like? Do you have people in your life with whom you can be vulnerable? Make a list of the people in your life you could tell anything. Do you share your successes and failures with them? Why or why not?

2. Are there people in your life who come to you with their "confessions"? How are you at listening to them? What strategies work effectively for you when listening to others? What dynamics make it a challenge?

3. What is the biggest barrier to being open and honest about your struggles?

4. What steps can you take to act in spite of to dissolve that barrier?

5. What are you most afraid of as you move forward? Do you believe that bringing your pain into the light will break that fear?

6. What is your strategy for dealing with that fear in a healthy way? Who will you talk about it with? Will your life look different without that fear?

CONSUMERISM

Let me start by asking you a couple of questions:

✳ What was the last thing you bought that wasn't a necessity?

✳ Why did you buy it? How did you make that choice?

✳ Have you ever said something was "cool"?

✳ How did it earn that distinction?

✳ Where do you think the concept of "cool" comes from, and how do you determine what is "cool" and what is not?

When you start answering questions like these, you begin to see the tangled web we call "consumerism." Consumerism for us is like the air we breathe. It is an economic, social, and (I will argue) religious system that surrounds us at all times in the United States. If we don't wake up to its influence, consumerism can actually be toxic. That's part of what motivated the group that goes to a franchise bookstore dressed as robots in the *Blue Like Jazz* movie. Their public demonstration was designed to be a wake-up call to the people in the store about the reality of consumerism and the dangers of not paying attention to it.

Let's try to break down what consumerism is, explore how we are influenced by it, and discuss how the gospel of Jesus Christ actually challenges its very powerful story about what matters most in life.

Our Take...
Consumerism: The Matrix That Is Everywhere

By definition, consumerism is a social and economic order based on the belief that it is good for a society and its individual members to buy and use large quantities of goods.[1] In this system, the individuals are seen as consumers and the whole enterprise is maintained by the perpetual creation of fresh needs. Consumers are motivated to buy the next new thing because the system works to engender a need they don't yet have. Sound familiar yet? People have been talking about this kind of arrangement as "consumerism" since the 1960s in the United States, but there is nothing new about this way of living. Many ancient societies from Babylon to Rome have abided by this same dynamic of buying and using more than their basic needs required, but it was usually limited to the wealthiest, most powerful, and most prosperous of a culture. However, when the Industrial Revolution[2] made products cheaper and more widely available through mass production, everything started to change. The working classes in the United States now had access to an increasing variety of goods and services, and the way of life now known as consumerism took off like a rocket. However, while industry and mass production might have been what built the rocket known as consumerism, what has fueled it is advertising.

Did you know that people in the United States are exposed to more than four thousand advertising images a day?[3] That's a staggering number—but if you really think about it, it's not so hard to imagine. Everywhere we go there are advertising images. Everywhere. There are the obvious ones like commercials in between TV programs, banner ads on Facebook, and billboards along the highway. But there are also more subtle ads like the products placed in movies, the cartoon characters on children's food packaging, and the brand names visible on the very clothing you might be wearing right now. That's right—if you are wearing a T-shirt or hat with a brand logo on it, you are doing the advertiser's job for them.[4] Pretty sneaky, huh? So how do they get away with all this?

Advertising works by identifying consumer needs and then providing products and services to meet those needs. Sometimes these needs are real and sometimes they are just plain made up. The most famous example of this is the story of the word *halitosis*. In the early 1900s, Listerine was looking for a new way to sell its patented mouthwash. To do this, its marketing team took the Latin word *halitus* (which means "breath") and combined it with the Greek suffix *-osis* to create a new name for a fairly common affliction—halitosis, otherwise known as "bad breath."[5] The advertisements told consumers that use of Listerine was their only hope against this dreaded affliction, and it worked like a charm. In fact, it worked so well that halitosis went from the newspaper ads of the 1930s all the way into the English lexicon proper. Today the term is so familiar that it's easy to forget it was advertisers who created it. But they did and the same dynamic continues today. In everything from skin care products to car commercials, advertisers want you to know that you are not happy or at peace unless you have bought what they are selling.

But if this is how consumerism works, it is certainly not the way we experience it.

Our actual experience of consumerism is a lot more like the 1999 movie *The Matrix*. In this film, Keanu Reeves plays Neo, a computer programmer who comes to realize that his whole life is actually a computer-generated fantasy called the Matrix. Laurence Fishburne plays Morpheus, a resistance leader who frees Neo and helps him "see the Matrix." This task is difficult at first because Neo has always accepted the Matrix, although it's simply a computer-generated dream. To help him understand, Morpheus explains: "The Matrix is everywhere. It is all around us. Even now, in this very room. You can see it when you look out your window or when you turn on your television. You can feel it when you go to work . . . when you go to church . . . when you pay your taxes. It is the world that has been pulled over your eyes to blind you from the truth."

Neo responds, "What truth?"

Morpheus continues, "That you are a slave, Neo. Like everyone else you were born into bondage. Into a prison that you cannot taste or see or touch. A prison for your mind."

In our culture today, consumerism is very much like the Matrix. It is all around us everywhere we go. And though it dictates our choices and tastes and affects the way we feel about our bodies, we are generally not aware of its influence. It is, as Morpheus says, "the world that has been pulled over our eyes" because we have never known life without it. Consumerism is what many consider "normal."

But what if it's not?

Religious Consumerism

Have you ever met someone who told you they were spiritual but not religious? This is a popular sentiment among folks who want to distance themselves from the abuses and confines of institutional religions, yet retain a connection to the transcendent. I get it—I really do. However, what many of these folks don't realize is that they often already have a religion—consumerism.

Religions are the stories, symbols, and practices that give human life meaning. They are the narratives that give us purpose and direction by helping us decode the big, big questions of life like, "Who am I?" "Why am I here?" and "Where am I going in life?" To all these questions, consumerism says, who you are and where you're going in life depends on what you buy. You can choose your life story by purchasing the right products. These products, in turn, will give you identity, meaning, and purpose. Such a promise is *religious* in nature. It holds out personal fulfillment and peace as something that can be had with just the right purchase. In this way, consumerism functions as a sort of folksy religion in our culture. It provides a story for making sense of who we are and where we are going in this world. Why else would Apple computers ask me, "What kind of iPod are you?" They want me to make a religious level of identification with their product by saying, "I am an *Apple* guy" in hopes that I will then go down to the store and buy one.

But let's take this religious consumerism one step further.

All religions have some sort of holiness code—meaning the external actions that demonstrate a worshiper's commitment to the faith. Consumerism's holiness code is without a doubt "coolness." The pursuit of "cool" is paramount in the consumer religion and also what keeps consumerism going because "cool" is a moving target. What is cool today is not what was cool last year and is not what will be cool tomorrow. This changing face of "cool" is not a natural phenomenon of course, but like *halitosis*, is part of a marketing system that it is crafted and sold to us season after season.[6] Nevertheless we chase it, feel alienated if we can't achieve it, and even resent those who have it. Sainthood in consumerism is achieved by reaching "coolness," which makes hipsters the religion's monks.[7] Yet even those who disavow popular notions of "cool" can be caught in the Matrix of it all.

I am a Generation X-er and remember being in college in the early 1990s when the cool thing to do was to buy clothes at the thrift store. This included vintage jeans, flannel shirts (it was the early '90s after all), and especially too-small T-shirts emblazoned with offbeat images and slogans. The more random the better. This was our way, we thought, of getting free of the consumer machine and determining our own style. We would take what was considered ugly by popular standards, embrace it ironically, and declare it to be "cool." But we weren't as free as we thought. Far from being liberated, our whole ironic-ugly-hip thing was still being shaped by the consumer religion, because we were striving to be cool. Yes, our practice began as an authentic alternative to what the market was saying we had to look like.[8] However, we were not leaving the consumer system at all because we were still trying to be "cool." Coolness was our temple—our holy table. It was an altar. An altar of cool.[9] And as long as we served at that altar, we were still "in the Matrix."

Christians have to call worship at the altar of cool what it is: idolatry.

The belonging, hope, and purpose offered by consumerism are in direct conflict with the gospel of Jesus Christ and we can't serve both masters. Jesus' teachings directly challenge the values of the consumer religion and its altar of cool. One of the most striking places this happens is in a parable Jesus told about a rich man who grows so much food that he has more than he can possibly need. When this man considers what to do with his surplus, he decides to tear down his old barns and build new, bigger ones. That way he can keep all of the harvest for himself. Jesus declared this man to be "a fool" and concluded the teaching by saying, "Life is [about] more than food, and the body is more than fancy clothes."[10] Or take God's command in Exodus for Israel not to covet.[11] This command is a call for God's people not to lust after what someone else has. God knows the slavery these types of cravings can be and how they drive us to darker places if we try to take what has not been given to us. Freedom is being thankful for what we have been given while coveting corrupts us into believing that we won't be happy until *we* have what *they* have.

Wait a minute! Really? Life is about more than food and the body more than clothes? Not according to my television! Coveting is a sin? It sounds like exactly what every commercial I've ever seen is trying to evoke in me. How can this contradict God's good order? I thought this is just the way things are!

It is the way things are, but not the way things have to be. We can live differently.

And herein lies the challenge for Christians living in a consumer culture. Can we sift out what our real needs are in a marketplace that is continually hammering us with the message that we don't have enough? How will we muster the courage and imagination it takes to live out the story of human purpose according to the gospel and not according to the matrix of consumerism? If you want to take this narrow road, keep reading. This next part is for you.

Unplugging from the Matrix of Consumerism

We have one of those DVRs that allows us to pause and record live TV. It's the neatest thing because it means I can skip the commercials—a perk that I love. Now, when my kids watch TV, sometimes they want to watch the commercials and I'm okay with that as long as they agree to talk to me about them afterward. Sometimes they are game for this, and sometimes not. Recently we watched an ad for breakfast cereal and I asked the kids, "Could you tell how they were selling that to you? What kind of person does that company think is going to buy their cereal based on the type of commercial they've made?" How did my children respond? With total annoyance! "Dad!" they exclaimed in exaggerated tones that came complete with eye rolling. "Don't make us talk about this again!" But as much as my kids may complain, we have to talk about this stuff because I will need their help in taking our lives a different direction.

Unhooking from consumerism is something we have to do together. It is about making intentional choices to live in new ways, and that takes communal effort. The centrifugal force of our culture will always pull us back into the consumer whirlpool, and to avoid the pull, we need the cooperation of other people and a plan. Where do we start such a plan? Here are a few ideas:

The first step in unplugging from the matrix of consumerism can be simply paying attention to the influence the system already has in your life. Spend one day trying to count the number of advertisements and brand names you see. Think about why you are buying what you are buying. Ask if you have considered the issues of justice connected to that item's production.[12] Make a note of what in your life makes it easy to see the consumer machine at work and what makes it hard. Then try to encourage one of the good things and dissuade one of the damaging ones.

The next step might be to intentionally turn away from the altar of "cool" for a season. Ask yourself: Do I chase cool? How hard do I work to stay "in fashion" or to ironically bend out of it? Am I even aware of the powerful yet corrosive force of irony?[13] Ask yourself how the cult of cool influences the choices you make about friendships, jobs, even where you live. Think about the character of Penny in *Blue Like Jazz*. When Don first meets her he discovers she has chosen to wear the same clothes for a year to protest both the unfair labor practices used to produce most clothing and the consumer machine that lusts for low prices. Are there ways you can creatively and sacrificially say no to the call of cool as well? Maybe it comes by doing one thing a week that "does not compute" according to the consumer machine. Intentionally keep and wear a piece of clothing that is out of style. Or choose not to buy a current piece of technology until what it is replacing actually wears out. Take the energy and time you would spend shopping (including surfing retail websites) and use it to serve the poor in your town. These are a few simple ways to begin unplugging from the consumer matrix, and I'll bet you will come up with better ideas of your own.

In all these things, remember to just focus on taking the right next step and don't give up. Our God is a God who likes to journey, and with the Spirit leading our trip out of consumerism, we can trust it will be a trip worth taking.

THE WAY IN . . .

Watch the section of the movie when Don and Penny go with other students dressed as robots into the bookstore, followed by Don's DVD clip on consumerism.

1. What is your reaction to this scene?

2. What do you think the student group is trying to accomplish with this demonstration? Is it effective?

3. Is this sort of activism appealing or unappealing to you?

4. How is what they are doing reflective of God's kingdom? How is it not?

5. Do you think advertising influences you? Why or why not?

6. Where do you see the most advertising in your life?

EXPLORING FURTHER . . .

1. How do you determine what is "cool"?

2. The author makes the case that consumerism is a type of religion. Do you agree? Why or why not?

3. Have you ever considered where the things you buy come from or how they are made? If so, give an example.

4. Are there any spaces you have that are free from advertising? What are they? If you don't how, can you create some?

5. The author says, "Sainthood in consumerism is achieved by reaching 'coolness,' which makes hipsters the religion's monks." Do you agree with this statement? Why or why not?

6. Is it wrong for Christians to be stylish or to wear clothes that are in fashion? How is that different or the same as consumerism?

CRAFTING YOUR RULE

1. Where do you see consumerism influencing your life the most?

2. Where do you see the most advertisements?

3. List three things you are already doing that society may consider "uncool."

4. In what areas does "the call of cool" appeal to you most? Can you come up with two "uncool" actions that would help you resist this call?

5. What will be the hardest part about unplugging from consumerism and the altar of cool?

6. Who can join you in this?

7. What are you most afraid of as you move forward?

8. What is your strategy for dealing with that fear in a healthy way? Who will you talk about it with? What will your life look like without that fear?

9. Pick one of the resources for further reading in the endnotes and explore it with a friend. Write down what you learn together and talk about helpful ways to share it with others.

CHAPTER 4

CULTURE

When you hear the word *culture*, what do you think of?
Or tougher yet, how would you define it? Really, take a minute and
think about it. It's not easy to do off the cuff, is it? There are lots of
things that we label as "culture" but what culture actually is includes
a bit of all of them. We call ethnic identities coupled with the social
and family systems that support them "culture" (think Hispanic or
African American culture here). We talk about trends in fashion,
music, and entertainment as "pop culture." The values and
ideologies of a society are defined as "culture" when we say things
like "the culture wars" or "the decline of our culture." Refined
tastes in the arts, literature, or humanities are sometimes called
"high culture," and let's not forget about what happens in a petri
dish. When something grows in there, that's called "culture" too.

None of the definitions are wrong, but taken on their own,
they only give a partial view of what culture is from a biblical
perspective. However, when taken together, they disclose a
beautifully panoramic picture of not only what culture is, but also
what Christians are supposed to think about it.

Our Take...

Conversations about culture and Christianity need to begin in that aforementioned biology class. The word *culture* comes from a Latin word *cultura*, which means literally "to cultivate." This makes culture, at its most basic level, something that is grown. Take the virus or bacteria growing in the lab for example. It is called a "culture" because the scientist is "cultivating" that living material. She is literally making something come to life within the goop. This is why the starting point for understanding culture is to remember that it is something people create.[1]

What's so cool about this is the way it echoes Adam and Eve's vocation in the garden of Eden.[2] When the Lord made the human beings, they were created in God's image to subdue and rule the creation. The intent of this command was not for humans to dominate the creation but to develop it.[3] This is part of what it means for people to be made in the image of God. They are tasked with making something good within the place God has made by continuing God's good work. So, our other expressions of culture—ethnic identities, social ideologies, arts, music, and the taste to appreciate them—all flow out of the God-given imperative to make. So, whether it's values, language, food, or film, the things people create are what makes up a culture; and creating culture is a God-blessed endeavor.

Of course, the problem with everything being created as good and God-blessed in Genesis 1 and 2 is that things are no longer the way they were supposed to be. Because of human rebellion, sin and death entered the good creation and everything that was made to be harmonious, healthy, and alive became infected with conflict, sickness, and decay. So, while some of the culture humans make is still the God-blessed kind, because of our post-Genesis 3 world, we are capable of making other kinds of culture as well.

One summer I joined a group of guys who played cards together every night. They were a great group of young men who were really fun to be with; however, there was one guy whom everyone teased mercilessly. He seemed to be the whipping boy of this crew, and before long I found myself making fun of him too. The more I teased him, the more accepted I felt, and before I knew it, I had fallen victim to one of the classic blunders—going along with the crowd even when it was the wrong thing to do. However, as I reflect on how I treated this guy all these years later, I am shocked that I ever started. He was part of the group before I was. What business did I have being rude to someone I didn't even know? And yet, because the group dynamic trended toward picking on him, it wasn't long before I joined right in. This whole fiasco is a small example of how the culture people make is not always good and God-blessed.[4]

So, while culture is something that is made and we were designed to make it, not all of our creations necessarily reflect the Creator, do they? We have great power and authority to choose the kinds of culture we make, which raises an interesting question: How should the Christians make culture? What is the right way for the people of God to make culture, and how do they create it so their culture bends toward the gospel and not away from it?

Christ and Culture

If you have ever wondered about the place of Christians in their culture, you're not alone. The church has wrestled with it for hundreds of years, and her attempts are most famously described in H. Richard Niebuhr's influential book *Christ and Culture*.[5] Written in 1951, Niebuhr's book surveys the landscape of church history and proposes five typologies for how the church has interacted with culture over the years.

Niebuhr called the first relationship between the church and culture "Christ Against Culture." This represents all Christians over the centuries who have believed that loyalty to Jesus meant total separation from the corrupting influence of their culture. This separation often manifested itself in groups of believers moving away from city centers to establish alternative societies as part of their Christian witness. In Jesus' day, the Essene movement best exemplified this. The Essene's loyalty to Yahweh demanded that they evacuate their corrupt, Roman-dominated culture. So they did, moving to the deserts of the Judean wilderness and setting up shop in places like Qumran.[6] This same sentiment can be found in the early church within the life of the Desert Fathers and Mothers and can be seen today in groups like the Amish.[7] "Christ Against Culture" assumes that culture inherently corrupts allegiance to Jesus and therefore demands that it be left behind.

Swinging to the opposite extreme is Niebuhr's next typology, "Christ of Culture." Here, the Christian message accommodates the culture such that the culture's values and standards actually change the Christian message. Niebuhr uses a heresy the early church called Gnosticism as his prime example of "Christ of Culture." Gnosticism was a product of Greek philosophy that asserted that your body was all bad, your spirit was all good, and you needed to acquire a secret knowledge (*gnosis* is the Greek word for "know," which is the root for *Gnosticism*) in order to escape the prison of your body and rise into a pure spiritual realm after your death. This belief system took many of the stories and symbols from the early Christian church and tried to claim that Jesus was a Gnostic. They even wrote their own accounts of Jesus' life, like the Gospel of Thomas or the Gospel of Judas, to try and further bolster their claims.[8] Gnosticism was a major problem for the early church because it denied Jesus' humanity. Fortunately, it was tamped down during the great ecumenical councils, but its allure certainly endures today. Whenever Christians seek relevance within their culture and unintentionally let the culture set the agenda "Christ of Culture" is in play.[9]

When the newly minted Roman emperor Constantine issued the Edict of Milan in AD 313, a new typology was born. Before the Edict, Christianity had been a seriously persecuted religion (think of being thrown to the lions here). However, after the Edict, Christianity wasn't just tolerated; it slowly became the official religion of the Roman Empire. Now instead of being a persecuted minority, the church was a state-backed majority, which is the premise of the "Christ Above Culture" typology. In "Christ Above Culture," the church is in charge and calling the shots in their culture. Some examples of this are the Holy Roman Empire and the denominationally backed Nation States of Europe after the Reformation. Most of the criticisms of Christianity's past (the Crusades, the Inquisition, the burning of heretics, to name a few) come from the time[10] when Christ was above culture.

Taking more seriously the difficulties that emerge when the church is at the center of the culture is "Christ and Culture in Paradox." This typology, built on the theology of Martin Luther, says that our current world is so sinful it is essentially beyond real redemption. However, instead of retreating from it, we need to split our world into two realms of existence: the secular and the sacred. The secular is the place where all things of the material world happen—business, economics, science, politics, art, music—while the sacred is where spiritual life takes place—church, prayers, worship. These two distinct realms of human existence coexist but do not overlap. Instead, they live in tension and give birth to familiar concepts like the separation of church and state.

Finally, and in an attempt to offer an alternative for his day, Niebuhr proposed "Christ Transforming Culture." In this typology, the church does not force her will on the culture ("Christ Above Culture"), retreat from the culture ("Christ Against Culture"), fail to critique the culture ("Christ of Culture"), or deem it a lost cause ("Christ and Culture in Paradox") but instead works to transform her culture to become a servant of the kingdom of God. This is accomplished as the church woos the culture into choosing Jesus of its own free will. When Christ transforms culture it happens through an invitation and not coercion. "Christ Transforming Culture" has been the preferred typology of many notable church figures like St. Augustine and John Wesley.

When I was first introduced to these five typologies, I thought I had to pick one like the whole thing was a multiple-choice test. I settled into "Christ Transforming Culture" because it resonated with both my experience as a youth minister and my conversations in church-growth circles.[11] I imagined that our job as God's people was to reach or impact our culture or even to save our culture for the sake of the gospel. However, I was missing one big truth: we don't transform culture; God does.

God alone is the one who, in Jesus, is rescuing and redeeming the world, not us. Jesus is the one who is making all things new, not me. So, when it comes to thinking about Christianity and culture, we have to start with the truth that God alone transforms, redeems, and heals culture. It's actually not the church's job; it's God's and God's alone.

Please don't misunderstand me. I'm not saying we as the church don't have a very important role to play. We do and I'll get to that in a moment. But our redemptive action must begin as a response to and support of God's. God is the one healing, repairing, and restoring all things, including our cultures, so our job is to join that activity. This is important to keep straight and it illustrates where the "Christ Transforming Culture" typology confused me. I read *Christ* transforming the culture as *church* transforming culture, which means I imagined our mission was to fight our culture and get it to change. And, while this is a noble goal, it is ultimately misdirected.[12] It forgets the place humans were created to have in this whole process, which is as culture makers.

God alone redeems culture. We, however, were designed to make culture that looks like our Creator, and this is precisely the part we are supposed to play. Christians are meant to partner with God's redemption by creating culture that reflects His kingdom.

This is our job, calling, and mission. But what does that look like and how is that done? I think it's a little like beating on a guitar.

Making Kingdom Culture

I remember the first time I heard the band Rage Against the Machine. I was in college and, being a musician myself, was instantly taken by lead guitarist Tom Morello. Not only were his riffs and musicianship first rate, but he also brought sounds out of the guitar I had never heard before. Synthesizing the styles of guitar heroes like Thurston Moore and Jimmy Page, Morello took his guitar and played it like a turntable in a hip-hop song.[13] His riffs and solos were alive with all kinds of squalls and scratches that he would manufacture by beating the guitar strings and playing with a shorted wire in his pick-up. I was awestruck by his approach to the instrument; how could someone take something I was so familiar with and make it sound brand-new? Morello found sounds that had been inside the instrument all along and brought them out for someone like me to enjoy.

This is precisely the approach that Christians should take making kingdom of God cultures. We are invited to use our creativity and ingenuity to find all of the right-side-up potential that has been there all along, and make it a present reality. This is what our God-given vocation to make culture looks like in practice. It's not to take over the culture, run from it, cow-tow to its whims, give up on it, or even transform it. Our job is to join God in building cultures that make things here on earth look like they do in heaven.

There is a ministry called Magdalene where I live in Nashville.[14] They provide a residential program for women who have survived lives of violence, prostitution, and addiction. Magdalene also runs a social enterprise called Thistle Farms, which produces bath and body products, the production of which helps gives their residents skills to make a new life for themselves.

Recently, my family volunteered to contribute some food to Magdalene's graduation reception. When my wife went to pick up the food we ordered at the deli, she suddenly felt moved by God to talk to the women assembling our cheese tray about what the food was for. Unsure of how to bring something like that up without sounding strange, my wife said, "Thanks so much for putting this tray together. It's for a graduation party for a ministry called Magdalene . . ." But before she could finish, one of the women behind the counter broke into a huge smile and said, "I'm in NA [Narcotics Anonymous] right now and I know *exactly* what Magdalene is all about. I was almost one of their residents." Then, with that same smile she passed the tray over the counter to my wife, said thank you, and went about her work.

When my wife came home she told me the story. She wasn't sure why she had been so moved by the experience. All she had done was share some information on a hunch that God may have been up to something. Because of this risk she ended up making a connection with someone who had been in a dark place and is now healed. However, it's actually much more than that. At a deeper level, in that moment, these two women made a new culture.

One of our definitions of culture is the ideologies and stories we live by in our world. The connection these two women made affirmed an alternative story about how the world works. A kingdom story. Their exchange acknowledged that death does not have the last word and that resurrection is true. They confirmed for one another that change really is possible for any and everybody because of this resurrection. And even more than that, these affirmations point to the truth that this world is going somewhere and God is really changing things. All that in fifteen seconds over a cheese tray.

I tell this story about culture making because of how small and unimpressive it is. Sure there are big and flashy examples of kingdom culture making where faithful men and women have established programs, institutions, and ministries that have made God-blessed culture in entire cities and countries. But these stories can leave us feeling overwhelmed if we're not the entrepreneurial type. There at the deli counter, these two women didn't change public policy or create a ministry to solve the world's hunger problems. They were faithful in one small thing—a conversation—and in their particular sphere, next to the rack of rotisserie chickens, over the cold cuts, things were as they were supposed to be. God's story of turning everything right-side up was proclaimed and heaven came to earth right then and there at Publix. The potential for this connection and revelation was there all along, but it took the brief exchange between the two women to make it a reality. I have a friend who calls this being a kingdom of God horticulturalist.[15] It is looking for the places God is bringing about His new world, and then when we see them, using our gifts to coax them forth and help them grow. Whether these changes are big or small is God's purview; our task is simply to be a faithful participant wherever we can, using our space to make good culture—even if cheese is involved.

This task of being a kingdom of God horticulturalist is now put to each of us. Culture happens. It is out there and we are a part of it. But how will we relate to it as Christians? Will we try to run from it? Will we give in to it? Will be give up on it? Will we try to control it? Or will we use the talent we have and the space we live in to join God by creating new kinds of culture? You already have everything you need to get started because you are already a culture maker. You're a person. The question is, what kind of culture will you make?

THE WAY IN . . .

Watch Don's DVD clip on culture.

1. What kind of cultures did you grow up in? Where do you see their influence on your life now?

2. Have you ever had an experience in a culture that was different than your own? How did it make you feel?

3. Why do you think people treat cultures that are different than their own as wrong?

4. What makes appreciating other cultures easy? What makes it hard?

5. How do you think cultures honor God?

EXPLORING FURTHER . . .

1. The author says there is no such thing as "*THE* culture." Do you agree? Why or why not?

2. When you hear the word *culture*, how do you define it? The author claims it is something people make. Do you agree?

3. Should Christians make "Christian culture" (meaning Christian versions of things)? In your opinion, is this practice helpful or unhelpful?

4. Do you resonate with the divison of our world into secular and sacred? Why or why not?

5. Where do you see Christ in our culture in places other than church?

6. What in the media (music, TV, movies) have you seen that demonstrates God's right-side-up world?

7. Which of the five typologies from *Christ and Culture* resonates the most with you? Is there one you grew up in? Are there any new ones we should add?

CRAFTING YOUR RULE

1. Use the space below and write down a working definition for culture.

2. Is it exciting or threatening to think about using your gifts to make culture changes?

3. What talents can you use to bring out the kingdom of God where you are?

4. What are you most afraid of as you move forward? Do you believe that bringing your pain into the light will break that fear?

5. What is your strategy for dealing with that fear in a healthy way? Who will you talk about it with? Will your life look different without that fear?

CHAPTER 5

DOUBT

I have a friend who is interested in God and extremely interested in Jesus. We talk about faith often, and our conversations are always open and honest. She knows that I'm "into the God kind of thing," yet when I suggest that we're not so different because she also seems to be "into the God kind of thing" too, the conversation always takes the same turn. "The difference between us," she explains, "is that, unlike you, I still have all these doubts." Unlike me? I have plenty of doubts. Does that negate my faith? Is faith something that comes only after all doubt is removed? Have you ever heard of this divide between faith and doubt? Have you ever wrestled with it yourself? What is the relationship between faith and doubt? Is one really the opposite of the other, or is there something deeper going on?

In high school and college you start to run into people who doubt things that are sacred to you. There will be those who doubt the traditional stuff like the existence of God, Christianity, and religion in general. You will also meet people with a robust skepticism as to the use and role of the government as well as the capacity of politicians to tell the truth (which may manifest itself in any number of conspiracy theories). However, you will also find that, as you mature, sometimes these doubts come from within. If it hasn't happened already, you may find yourself doubting elements of your own life and faith. Doubt will be part of your life experience with God eventually. The question is, does doubt have to be a deal breaker? Is the only way to make sense of doubt to ignore it and pretend it doesn't exist, or is there a more helpful way to engage it? I think there is. In fact, I would go so far as to say that doubt is actually *part of* faith and in many ways, faith cannot exist without doubt. We therefore have to learn not how to eliminate doubt but how to doubt well. This kind of good doubt can actually lead to new understanding, deeper friendships, and a renewed faith. However, to get there we will first need to explore where our modern concept of doubt comes from.

Our Take...

We live in a time that is transitioning between two philosophical worldviews. The view that has shaped everything for the last five hundred years or so is called modernity. Have you ever heard of it? Modernity has some very particular contours and owes much of its heritage to the philosophy of a guy named René Descartes. If you have ever heard the phrase "I think, therefore I am," then you already know a little about Descartes. This was his major philosophical innovation and it changed everything.

Descartes lived during his own time of change and transition. The medieval ways of coming to knowledge (in a philosophical sense) just weren't working for Descartes anymore. He needed to explore some new possibilities but wanted something that was sure and certain—a foundation he could construct a new philosophy upon. To find this he settled on a process of questioning everything he knew, digging deeper until he got farther and farther down into the bedrock of all his assumptions. After much internal struggle, Descartes found that the only thing he could not doubt was the fact that he was doubting. He doubted (read "thought"), therefore he could know that he existed. *Cogito ergo sum*—"I think, therefore I am." This concept became the foundation Descartes was looking for and from it, he built a whole new way of knowing things.[1]

Descartes's philosophy kick-started the European Enlightenment and had a major influence on the scientific revolution that followed. As the scientific method and its penchant for eliminating possibilities through objective questioning gained authority and confidence in the eighteenth and nineteenth centuries, so did doubt as the starting place for gaining knowledge. If you wanted to know if something was true in modernity, you needed to doubt it.

How all this works out in reality can be illustrated in a card game I used to play on family vacations called "I Doubt It." The way the game worked was that all fifty-two cards were dealt out evenly among the players and then, following numerical order (ace, two, three, four, etc.) each player lays at least one card of the number that falls to them face down declaring to everyone what it is. So, if the first player has one ace, they would lay it face down in the middle of the table saying, "One ace." Play continues with the next player laying down however many twos he has, the next player plays his threes, and so on until someone gets rid of all their cards. When they do they win.

What made me love this game as a kid is what happened if a player did not have a card of the required number in their hand. They would just pick a random card (or cards if they were brave), lay them on the table face down, and lie through their teeth telling everyone as convincingly as possible that it was the card being asked of them. However, if someone gets wise to the lie before the next card is laid down, they could say, "I doubt it!",[2] at which point the card last laid down is revealed. If the player was indeed lying, then he must put all the cards from the center of the table into his hand. If he was telling the truth, the one who doubted him must take all the cards.

When someone doubts in the game, it comes with a "guilty until proven innocent" tone. "I doubt it!" They do not believe the doubtee is telling the truth and are unwilling to take the claims made about the card laid on faith. The burden of proof is then placed on the doubtee to provide some objective, indubitable piece of evidence in answer to the doubt claim. So, they turn the card over and, when the truth is objectively revealed, one player is rewarded and the other punished.

This is just a microcosm of the weird expectations we bring to the concept of doubt in our day, isn't it? Thanks to Descartes, we have come to doubt as a path to knowledge, but an unintended consequence has been the way faith has become its enemy. It's as though modernity turned the culture into a big game of "I Doubt It," where people making faith claims are trying to get away with something and doubt is the only way to get to the real truth of the matter. The sad part is that the church has played right along with the whole affair. I work with a student at a private Christian high school, and we often discuss his struggles with his Christian faith. His tensions are not with the content of the faith but instead with the fact that he has any questions at all. At his school, he feels that he is not allowed to ask questions about faith. He told me recently that doing so is frowned upon because, "If you have doubts, people look at you like there's something wrong with you, like you don't have a strong enough faith. When I tried to talk about my doubts at school I was just given more doctrine. So, I eventually stopped talking about anything at all."

Is this how it has to be? Is doubt really the opposite of faith? Does the existence of one mean the rejection of the other? I don't think so. What if faith and doubt are not opposite but actually coexist in all of us? What if they are interdependent and not exclusive?

What if doubt and faith don't fight, but instead dance?

Doubt and Faith: Let's Dance

The reason faith and doubt have occupied so many of the same philosophical conversations for the past five hundred years is because they go together. Doubt is a necessary component of faith because faith involves risk. It requires the possibility that the believer may be wrong. I'm not trying to say faith is wrong or that it is absurd to have faith or anything like that. All I'm trying to say is that when you put your faith in something, there is a trust required that acknowledges yet transcends your doubts. Danish philosopher Søren Kierkegaard put it this way: "Belief is not a decision based on evidence that says certain beliefs about God are true. No such evidence could ever be enough to justify the kind of total commitment involved in true theological belief. Belief involves making that commitment anyway."[3] We grow in our faith not in spite of our doubts, but because of them.[4] That's why any security we experience in our faith comes not from certainty but from what one theologian calls a proper confidence.[5] It reminds me of the attitude Peter and the disciples had after Jesus ran the crowds off by telling them they must eat His body and drink His blood. Complaining of the difficulty of this teaching, the masses walked away, and then Jesus turned to the Twelve and asked, "Do you want to walk away too?" Peter responded, "Lord, if we were to go, who would we follow? You speak the words that give everlasting life."[6] I feel that. It may not make sense all the time, the teaching may be hard, and we may have our doubts about whether we can make it or if the whole thing is crazy, but where else are we going to go? Jesus, You have the words of eternal life.

So, let's stop talking about doubt and faith as though they are two MMA fighters entering the octagon to do battle to the death. Instead, let's view them as dancing partners. Faith is leading, but if doubt does not follow her lead, the dance of belief will fall apart. Each needs the other because they cannot do it alone. Take either partner away and there is no dance.

This dance of faith and doubt helps to make sense of one of the stranger stories in the gospel of Mark.[7] In Mark 9, a father brought his son to Jesus and asked him to heal the boy of an impure spirit. He explained to Jesus that the boy had been like this all his life and that the spirit propeled the boy into water and fire, trying to kill him. He was desperate for his son's safety and said to Jesus, "But if there's anything You can do, please, have pity on us and help us." Here is the commingling of faith and doubt. The father believed enough to bring his boy, in all his pain and torment, to Jesus but was still not certain Jesus would heal him. He had heard about Jesus' healing ministry, but knew that not everyone who sought healing received it. So in his doubt he said, "But *if* there's anything You can do, please, have pity on us and help us."

Jesus responded, "What do you mean, '*if* there's anything'—all things are possible, if you only believe," to which the boy's father said, "I believe Lord. Help me to believe!"

I do believe. Help my unbelief? Well, which is it? It's a simple question, right? Either you believe or you don't. No, what this man is doing is making a creedal confession about Jesus that includes both belief and unbelief. Faith and doubt—together—in his one confession of trust. And do you know how Jesus responded? He healed the boy! Can doubt and faith actually work together to make the kind of belief that brings the healing of heaven to earth? I think so.

Bad Doubt

So, what matters in life is not avoiding doubt. No one can do that. What matters is how we choose to deal with our doubt when it crops up. Doubt is not inherently bad or inherently good. It's just a question of how it can be worked toward ends that are healthy and redemptive and not sick and destructive. What makes doubt good or bad is not its presence, but its outcome.

Many emerging adults have their worldviews challenged for the first time when they go to college or get their first job in the grown-up world. Being confronted with new ideas, religions, or just plain old-fashioned tragedy (like Don experiences in the movie) can rattle our cages and challenge some of our most sacredly held assumptions. Sadly, I've seen many EAs run into a patch of doubt and decide that the response is to dive into all sorts of unhealthy life choices. These are the EAs who have not been taught how to deal with doubt well.

Imagine a student who grows up in a household where Christianity and alcohol do not go together. The first month of her freshman year, she meets some upper classmen who are Christians and drink alcohol and she learns that not only did Jesus drink wine but so does the Presbyterian elder who teaches her introduction to the Bible class. All this brings a moment of doubt into her life. She has been taught only one perspective, and now that she has new information to process, the question becomes: What will she do with this new knowledge?

Bad doubt can lead this student to scrap the faith she was raised in and jump both feet into full-blown partying. She takes the tension the doubt is causing, and instead of exploring her faith, she uses the doubt as license to misbehave. At first she only drinks on weekends, but soon, even though she's not of age, she starts going out on Thursday nights too. Pretty soon she's telling herself that as long as she's not drinking two weekdays in a row, she doesn't have a problem even though the growing list of people she is alienating with her behavior might disagree. This is bad doubt. This is a doubt that produces nothing beneficial and is used as an excuse to indulge in self-destructive and consumer-driven pleasure seeking.

Good Doubt

Good doubt, on the other hand, will disrupt the standard account of our lives but cause us to ask new questions about ourselves and our world.[8] Good doubt is not the end of faith, or a license to live selfishly, but instead is the beginning of new understanding. Good doubt can actually build a community instead of taking someone into selfish isolation.

Philosopher/pastor/author Pete Rollins has a great saying: "To believe is human but to doubt is divine."[9] What Pete is getting at begins with theologian G. K. Chesterton. In his classic work *Orthodoxy*, Chesterton asserted that on the cross, Jesus became an atheist.[10] The moment He cried, "My God, My God, why have You forsaken Me?" Jesus doubted His God-ness. He was stripped of all His identity and dignity in a moment of ultimate doubt. On the cross, the God of the universe doubted His own divinity. Rollins contends this pattern is to be followed by all who take up their cross and follow Jesus.

Take, for example, the false identities we construct all the time. We want to see ourselves in certain ways, so we put our most flattering pictures on Facebook, list the books we want everyone to know we've read, and "like" the causes and groups that make us look the best. We work hard to project the image of who we want others to think we are instead of being who we really are. The Christian faith, says Rollins, will doubt these false identities. The Holy Spirit will disrupt our attempts to maintain these false identities because they are a prison. They are a slavery that keeps us from telling the truth about who we really are so we doubt them as a path to freedom.

This is what good doubt looks like. Questioning that manifests itself not in objective criticism but in authentic self-reflection. It happens when we catch a glimpse of how our lives actually line up with what we say we believe and have to confront any discrepancies. It's one thing to say we know that money does not lead to happiness. However, if the motivations of your life are driven by the state of your bank account, the quality of your clothes, or whether or not you have a cool cell phone, it does not matter what you say you believe. You are living as if something else is true. How does your belief system line up with your actual life choices? Taking the time to honestly answer that question can lead to the best kind of doubt indeed.

This is where community comes into play. Asking probing questions about the consistency of your character is one thing, but what about when the doubt you experience comes as a result of tragedy? This sort of doubt can really do a number on us. Maybe a family member commits suicide, a friend dies in a car accident, or one of our peers gets cancer. These kinds of events rattle us to our core. They will cause us to doubt things like God's goodness and mercy. We find ourselves asking age-old questions from a place of deep pain like, "How can a good God allow suffering to exist?"

Surprisingly, this doubt can be good, because it makes space for our faith communities to come alongside us, pick us up, and say, "You haven't got any faith right now? That's okay. You can borrow some from us." Our churches are there to carry us in our low moments, not because they want to control our lives but because they love us. This is the fruit of good doubt—an interdependent community of faith, bearing each other's burdens and loving one another precisely as Jesus loved us all. Even at our lowest moments we can make our doubt good when we allow ourselves to be carried.

So, when doubt happens, don't panic. It's not the end of the world; rather it might just be the beginning of faith. Don't ignore your doubt; explore it. Use it as an excuse to dig deeper into your faith, and to learn more about the God who loves you so much. Stay with the people you love and trust, those who bring out the best in you, so that when you doubt, you will doubt well. Resist the urge to go on a bender because "now there's no meaning" anymore. You are smarter than that. That is bad doubt. Use your doubt to make something beautiful (like deepened friendships and increased trust). If God can bring resurrection and an entire new creation out of the horror of the cross, He can certainly help us make new life out of our doubts. So, go forth and doubt boldly—in Jesus' name!

THE WAY IN . . .

Watch Don's DVD clip on doubt.

1. Is there a time when you can remember doubting your faith? If so, when was it?

2. Why do you think doubt is such a difficult thing for Christians to deal with?

3. How have you seen people deal well with doubt?

4. Don said the key to dealing with doubt is not to overreact and to take the long view. Have you ever had any success with taking the long view? If so, when? Have you ever overreacted?

EXPLORING FURTHER . . .

1. The author contends that doubt is not the opposite of faith; certainty is. Do you agree?

2. Respond to Peter Rollin's quote that "To believe is human, but to doubt is divine." Do you think this is true? How is doubt divine?

3. Write or tell a story about a time you've seen bad doubt happen in a person's life. What is happening in that person's life now?

4. Write or tell about a time you've seen good doubt happen in a person's life.

5. Where are you most prone to doubt?

CRAFTING YOUR RULE

1. Is there any place you are holding on to beliefs so tightly that it may be hard to doubt in a productive way?

2. What would bad doubt look like in your life? Where do you think you would be prone to act badly?

3. What makes good doubt a challenge for you?

4. Who are the people in your life you can borrow faith from if
   you need it? Make a plan to ask them to be there for you if the
   going gets tough.

5. Is there something you are afraid might happen if you doubt
   certain things? Is there anyone who would not support you if
   you doubted certain things?

6. Who will you talk about this with? What if your worst fears are
   realized? Can you imagine still being okay?

CHAPTER 6

DRUGS

As strange as it sounds, my earliest exposure to drugs came from the 1984 movie *The Terminator*. I remember seeing it on television one Sunday afternoon and being totally captivated by a scene where the main character, a robot from the future called the Terminator gets shot in the chest and punches through a car windshield while trying to catch the film's heroine. Later in the film, the police are discussing how this could be possible, and because the perpetrator being a cyborg from the future isn't on the short list of possibilities, their talk turns to drugs. One officer muses, "He was probably on PCP. Broke every bone in his hand and wouldn't feel it for hours." When I heard this I remember thinking to myself, *There is something I can take into my body that will make me immune to pain? How do I get some of that?*

Clearly my logic shows that I was both too young for the movie and naïve when it came to the substances I would later learn were called "hard drugs." Hard drugs have a direct effect on the central nervous system. They are highly addictive, damaging the user through their usage,[1] and often ruin lives. These are drugs like cocaine, heroin, crack cocaine, methamphetamines, LSD, and even marijuana (more on this later). Soft drugs, on the other hand, include items like alcohol, tobacco, and caffeine. These drugs tend to have less potential for damage in the lives of users and are minimally addictive, earning them the designation "soft."

As I got older, I started to notice that the line between hard and soft drugs was not as clear as I had once thought. In high school chemistry class, I learned that both aspirin and ibuprofen directly affect the central nervous system. Moreover, I had experienced the effects of addiction to soft drugs like caffeine and alcohol to realize that the distinctions of "hard" and "soft" didn't work as well as they once did. Was there another way to evaluate our ethical choices regarding drugs, especially as a Christian? Indeed. That is where we are headed.

Statistically, the nation's leading drug problem is not with opium, crack, cocaine, or heroin. No, from a numbers standpoint the two most abused controlled substances among emerging adults are marijuana and the non-medical use of prescription painkillers.[2] In many of the conversations I've had about drugs with high school and college students, this seems to be a sticking point. It's usually easy for emerging adults to reach a consensus about the damaging effects of so-called hard drugs. They are powerfully addictive, and frequently destroy the body and mind. Because of their undeniable damaging effects and the fact that they can lead to death either by long-term abuse or overdose, most emerging adults agree that hard drugs should remain illegal—with one exception. The tone of the conversation changes when it comes to marijuana. Once pot is being discussed, the questions become, "How is marijuana any different than alcohol or caffeine?" and, "Is it really more addictive[3] or worse for you than trans fats or processed foods?" Also, the case is made that smoking marijuana should be permissible because, while it is presently illegal in many states, it shouldn't be. "You speed sometimes, don't you, Dixon?" I was once asked. "What's the difference between you breaking the law with your car and me breaking the law with my body? Isn't smoking pot a victimless crime?"

The thing is, these are actually really good questions. They represent more than simply adolescent push back. Instead they rightly point out some of the inconsistencies in our legal and moral standards about drugs. Christian conversations about drugs will require better categories than "hard and soft" and better strategies than "Just Say No." With this in mind, I'd like to explore a relational way of approaching drugs through the lens of the most confusing of them all—marijuana. Statistically speaking, this is the one you are going to be most tempted to use but will have the least helpful tools for addressing. So, allow me to make a Christian case for abstaining from marijuana—at least while it's still illegal.

Our Take...
Won't You Be My Neighbor?

One of my mentors in college was named Whis. Whis was a hippie and frequently told stories about his time in the counter-culture revolution of the late 1960s. One story he told was specifically about his time as an undergraduate when he used to sell pot and other drugs. Having grown up in the church, Whis had heard Jesus' teaching to "love your neighbor as yourself" and thought it was a pretty cool idea. So, he decided he would give drugs away to all his friends because that's what he would want them to do for him! This is how he wanted to love his neighbor as himself—by giving them drugs for free.

Is there anything wrong with this picture?

Is this what Jesus meant?

Not exactly.

Giving drugs away, while technically generous, is not very loving for two reasons. First, handing out substances that can addict, hurt, and even kill others is not showing them love—even if drugs are what they ask for. Showing love involves seeking the benefit, healing, and wholeness of another person. It puts their needs above your own and can even act as a catalyst to pull them into a better future than they would find on their own. Doling out illegal drugs certainly does not fit this paradigm. However, the second and bigger reason that Whis's choices missed Jesus' mark was because he was operating with too small a definition of who his "neighbor" was. His neighbors were not just the people he was selling drugs to but also the people who were making and distributing them as well.

In Luke 10:25–37, Jesus was teaching and a teacher of the Law (someone equivalent to a PhD in biblical studies, so someone who really knows their stuff) asked Him, "What must I do to experience the eternal life?" Jesus responded, "What is written in the Hebrew Scriptures? How do you interpret their answer to your question?" The teacher replied that the Law teaches to love God with all you've got and love your neighbor as yourself. Jesus agreed: "Follow these commands," He said, "and you will live."

However, because this was a pretty simple answer, the teacher pressed Jesus further: "Ah, but who is my neighbor?" In response, Jesus told a story about a man who is robbed, beaten, and left half dead while traveling the road between Jerusalem and Jericho. Two religious leaders pass him by without helping him and then one of Israel's most despicable enemies, a Samaritan,[4] picks him up, administers first-aid, takes him to a hotel where he can convalesce, and pays for all his expenses.[5]

At the end of the story, Jesus asked the teacher of the Law who, in the story, was a neighbor to the man? The teacher responded, "The one who showed mercy to him." Jesus then said, "Well then, go and behave like that Samaritan." Wait, what just happened? The original question that prompted Jesus' story was "Who is my neighbor?" but when the story was over, it was clear that the neighbor in the story is Israel's enemy! The Samaritan. In Jesus' kingdom, the person you find the most disgusting and undeserving of love is precisely the person you must love as you would love yourself. This is how to take part in God's new, right-side-up world. Loving even your enemies! Jesus had just taken the boundaries for who counts as a neighbor and opened them up as far as they can go. "Who is my neighbor?" the teacher asked Jesus. "Who isn't?" He replied.

This definition of who our neighbor is opens up new ethical dilemmas in a world that seems to be getting smaller and smaller every day. Thanks to technological advances in the way we communicate, do business, and travel, we have become increasingly aware of how interconnected our lives are with everyone else on the planet. In recent years, this interconnection has manifested itself economically. Take, for example, the economic reverberation that occurred globally in 2008, when U.S. investment banks began to fail. Those failures disrupted the economies of not just other corporations around the world, but entire countries as well. We must remember that this interconnection is not limited to the big, public affairs. It is also present in our most everyday and personal purchases. For example, my kids can buy T-shirts for six dollars at a big box retailer because there is someone overseas in a factory making that T-shirt where six U.S. dollars will cover that factory's overhead and pay their employees. In the best cases, this arrangement provides a fair wage for hard-working people to live on. However, in the worst cases, it can encourage the exploitation of factory workers (especially children) in service of keeping those costs down on my daughter's T-shirt.

For Christians, this reality (and others like it) has to be included in our conversations about who our neighbor is. Following Jesus' teaching means I'm compelled to consider (to the best of my ability) whether or not my purchases have a loving effect on the lives of the women and men who make what I'm buying. This is where I believe Whis's understanding of "neighbor" was too small and where Christians need to look when making choices about drugs. The effect of the drugs on Whis's friends was negligible compared to the effect his participation in the drug production industry had on the people making, shipping, and distributing those drugs. This business is so cruel, violent, and unjust that no Christian can take part in it (either by buying or selling) and love their neighbor as themselves.

This point was driven home for me when I was visiting a friend in Juarez, Mexico, in 2001. Together, he and I were going to visit an orphanage on the outskirts of town. Once we cleared the last of the neighborhoods, my friend pulled the car over and pointed to a cleared depression in the desert about fifty yards off the highway.

"You see that spot there? The police discovered a mass grave there last month. There were more than twenty bodies buried in it."

"What happened to them?" I asked.

"Drugs," he answered. "They were shot by a rival cartel in Juarez. And things just seem to be getting worse."

Sadly, he was more right than he knew. Ten years later, Juarez has devolved into utter chaos. The police and state governments have lost control of the city with two cartels competing for power using public beheadings, kidnappings, and murder to enforce their will. In 2010, the cartels tried to assassinate Juarez's chief of police, began to target drug rehabilitation clinics, and worse yet, started employing children as young as eleven to act as both couriers and, sickeningly, assassins.[6]

Sadly, all of this unrest and violence is over access to the drug-smuggling corridor that gets their product into the United States. They are murdering, terrorizing, and stripping even children of their humanity so that Americans can buy anything from a gram of cocaine to a dime-bag of marijuana. That grave I saw in Juarez was just the tip of the iceberg, and it drove home for me that there is nothing victimless about the crime of drug use. People are dying, and not just the people involved in organized crime but innocent people as well. All so citizens of the U.S. can get high. This is a perverse, inexcusable reality that demands action, which is why, for Christians, our action, should begin with abstinence. This is how we can begin to love our neighbor as ourselves—by not paying into the economics of the cartels. What drives the violence in Juarez is money, plain and simple. So, the most simple and immediate way to be part of the solution to this problem is to abstain from using drugs—including marijuana.[7]

In order to fully love our neighbors as we love ourselves, Christians must refrain from smoking marijuana.

Breakin' the Law! Breakin' the Law!

"Okay, Dixon, I hear what you're saying about drugs and all this justice stuff, and I agree. But what if I grow my own marijuana? Then it's not part of that system you were talking about and I'll be good, right?"

It is true that "growing your own" would avoid the violent system of drug trafficking, but one problem remains: in the United States, recreational use of marijuana is still illegal.

"Yes, Dixon, but it shouldn't be. It's different than cocaine or meth in so many ways, not the least of which being that it's a plant. It grows in the earth. How is marijuana any more unhealthy to smoke than tobacco or any more unhealthy than alcohol or processed foods?"

These are good questions and they have some merit. I agree that marijuana lives in a different zone than chemically engineered drugs. It is indeed a plant, and while I wouldn't recommend taking that too far (there are plenty of plants that will kill you if you smoke or eat them—tobacco being one of them) it is a different kind of thing than, say, heroin. Also, its effects, while still powerful, are more on par with alcohol and about as addictive as certain types of fatty foods. However, the fact remains that pot is illegal, which *does* set it apart from alcohol, tobacco, and even junk food, and Christians need to respect that fact.

Now, before you think I'm suggesting that the church should unquestioningly enforce the will of the state in some sort of unholy theocratic union, let me be clear—it is precisely because the church *must* at times challenge the authority of the state that Christians today should respect the current laws relating to marijuana.

Here is what I mean . . .

There is a long and noble list of Christians breaking the law for the sake of the gospel. Beginning in Judaism, extending throughout the ministry of Jesus Himself,[8] and continuing throughout church history,[9] God's people have sometimes had to push back when the law of the land limits, stifles, or obstructs God's justice. To say it another way, sometimes laws can keep the world upside down instead of allowing God's people to work with the Spirit in making it right-side up again. When this is the case, Christians are sometimes called to intentionally violate said laws and bear their consequences as a way of exposing their injustice. However, when the church does this, she historically has something very particular in mind: the benefit of others. Jesus followers engage in civil disobedience not so they can get a treat they feel they've been deprived of but because someone is suffering and God's right-side up way of things demands they go free.

This is why, in my opinion, pot's illegality still makes it off limits for Christians—even if they grow their own. Perhaps it should not be (and maybe it will not always be[10]), but for now it is. As such, Christians should hang back on using it because this is not one of those places where the church needs to break the law. Our "right" to smoke a joint is not where we play that card. Laws and governments can be part of God's good ordering of the new creation. They can play a part in making things right-side up and as such, need to be respected in their first offering. However, because the governments of this world are not the same as the kingdom of God, Christians should always be listening to the Spirit to evaluate the laws of the land: Are these laws part of the problem or part of God's solution?

The most obvious example of this in recent history is the civil rights movement in the United States. Martin Luther King Jr. was compelled by his Christianity to stand up against laws and statutes in the United States that oppressed African Americans and relegated so many to second-class citizenship. King and other civil rights leaders organized systematic law breaking in places such as lunch counters and busses so as to expose the oppressive nature of these laws, sometimes paying the ultimate price in the process. Here the church challenged the injustice of the state through the power of love and self-sacrifice. They broke the law to the glory of God. Using marijuana is not an issue of justice on the grand scale of civil rights, which is why, in my opinion, Christians should not use pot nor expend their energies trying to legalize it.[11] Respecting the current prohibition of marijuana and other drugs gives us integrity to challenge other laws when, like Dr. King, we must do what is right instead of what is easy.[12]

Why Did You Get Married?

In this conversation, marijuana presents the most confusing set of circumstances, because it seemingly exists in a gray area. This is because pot doesn't seem to fit the limited definition of hard or soft drugs, and some states are even legalizing the substance. The author contends that marijuana should be abstained from for two primary reasons. First, the injustice of the drug trade makes it impossible to participate in that economic system and still follow Jesus' teaching to love our neighbors as ourselves. Second, the current laws prohibiting recreational marijuana should not be broken because it compromises the church's witness and authority to challenge other areas of true legislated oppression. That being said, it is important to leave a conversation about drugs with this question: "Why does anyone want to get high in the first place?"

One of the best movies of the 1990s was Cameron Crowe's *Jerry Maguire*. Tom Cruise plays the title role as a sport agent who, because of a crisis of conscience, puts all his chips on his last and only client, fictional NFL wide receiver Rod Tidwell. The stress this puts on Jerry is part of the drama of the film as is the tension the audience feels when Jerry impulsively marries his assistant—a single mom with a young son. Everyone, including Rod Tidwell, wonders if this marriage happened for all the right reasons.

Shortly after the wedding, Jerry begins traveling with Rod to all his football games, and one night in the stadium parking lot after a game, Rod (who has a passionate relationship with his wife) challenges Jerry:

ROD. Go home to your wife.

JERRY. What's that supposed to mean?

ROD. What are you doing here?

JERRY. Giving you personal attention.

ROD. You don't want to go home.

JERRY. What?

ROD. I'm just trying to talk to you. How's your marriage? The husband and wife thing. How is that?

JERRY. Not everyone has what you have.

ROD. Why did you get married? I'm just asking as a friend.

JERRY. You want an answer? Loyalty . . . she was loyal. Everything . . . grew from there. It just . . . grew from there.

ROD. That's an answer?

JERRY. That's the answer.

Jerry doesn't want to go home because he's avoiding something. What he's avoiding comes to light throughout the rest of the film, but if he can stay on the road, he doesn't have to face it. If he doesn't think about why he got married, he doesn't have to acknowledge that maybe things are not as they should be in his life and he can avoid exploring his own deep-seated issues.

Sometimes, we do the same thing. Often, we are tempted to use drugs because we don't want to think about why we "got married." We don't want to look at the things in our past. Old hurts. Unforgiveness. Things done to us and left undone by us. These can be difficult and painful to face and can sometimes provide a reason, even subconsciously, for why we want to get high.

So, ask yourself before you use any drugs, legal or illegal, "Why do I want to use this? Am I running away from something that I should be facing? Am I avoiding something that needs to be addressed?" Healing is not the same as escaping, and if you are running from something, there is no high that will ever make it go away. However, though we cannot escape our pain, it can be redeemed. This is what our God does, and He is good at this sort of thing.

Lastly, remember, even if you are not running from pain or avoiding past mistakes, inviting illegal and hard drugs into your life can create serious problems for you and those who love you. As much as we've explored the gray areas of this conversation, the reality of addiction, abuse, and death that surrounds so many of these substances is incontrovertible. Please stay away from them and then build a strategy for dealing with drugs that will help you navigate legal and illegal substances, both hard and soft, in a way that loves God with everything you've got, and enables you to wholly love your neighbor as you love yourself.

THE WAY IN . . .

Watch Don's DVD clip on drugs.

1. Why do you think people use drugs?

2. Don asks if you might be getting high to avoid things. Does this observation resonate with you and your experience of people who use drugs?

3. Have you or anyone you know ever experienced addiction to any drugs? How did that affect you?

4. Can people be addicted to other things besides drugs? What kinds of things? What are the effects?

EXPLORING FURTHER . . .

1. What's the difference between a drug like cocaine and a drug like caffeine?

2. Why does the author say that drugs are not a victimless crime? Do you agree?

3. The author says, "Sometimes laws can keep the world upside down instead of allowing God's people to work with the Spirit in making it right side up again." What examples of this can you think of from modern and ancient history?

4. Summarize the author's two arguments for why Christians should abstain from marijuana.

CRAFTING YOUR RULE

1. Do you plan to use illegal drugs? Why or why not?

2. What will be the biggest temptation for you to use drugs inappropriately (the temptation to escape, social pressure, etc.)?

3. What are two strategies for addressing that temptation beyond "Just Say No."

4. Who will you invite into your life to help you?

5. Is there anything you are afraid of in regard to drugs?

6. What can you do to work through that fear?

CHAPTER 7

EVANGELISM

During my second year of seminary, I traveled down south to attend my cousin's wedding. Her reception was held in a big hotel located right in the middle of the city's revived Main Street. When the goings got slow at the reception, I headed street-side to people watch and have a cigar with my brother. When he ran back to his room, I noticed two guys approaching groups of shoppers and club goers on the other side of the block. By the time they got to me, it was clear what they were up to—they were evangelizing.

As they approached me, one of them asked, "If you died tonight do you know where you would spend eternity?" I was taken aback by the abrupt and direct nature of the question, and I found it hilarious that they were evangelizing a guy in divinity school. "I think so . . . I'm a Christian," I responded wryly, trying to hint that even though their Christian expression was not the same as my own we were all part of the same extended family. However, that didn't seem to matter. After giving my appearance a once over (I had long hair and was smoking), the older of the two men pressed me. "Are you sure? Because the apostle Paul says . . ." and he began quoting the epistles to me. As he spoke, a shocking realization set in—they didn't believe me. Because I didn't look like their definition of a Christian, they had already made up their minds about me. My response to their initial question didn't matter because I still seemed to be "unsaved" in their eyes. I tried to share this realization with them, but they just kept insisting I take the comic book–styled tract they were offering. Once I finally took it, they moved on and I was extremely frustrated. They hadn't seemed to listen to anything I said and as a result, in their minds, I was just another hell-bound lost soul, even though I was pretty sure the youth group I led would disagree.

Stories like this are what come to mind when you hear the word *evangelism*, right? The term conjures images of screaming street preachers, picket signs, and strangers asking you, "Where will you spend eternity?" Although I knew these stereotypes existed, it wasn't until I went to college that I saw where they came from. Every month, soap-box preachers, Christian drama teams, and folks running surveys about my "spiritual interests" set up shop outside the student union, all with the same goal—to evangelize the lost.

If you spend any time on a college campus, you are going to run across this kind of thing, and the impression it leaves is the reason many Christians have an allergy to the word *evangelism*. I've even been in circles of church leaders who, when the word *evangelism* comes up, just roll their eyes and assure us that they don't do that kind of thing. My question is, why do all the rude and inappropriate tactics used by some as an attempt to convert people get to define the word *evangelism* for the rest of us? Evangelism has a much deeper and longer history than that, and I'm not sure that I'm ready to give it up yet. There's something there to be mined. Furthermore, like it or not, evangelism is an inescapable part of the Christian faith. All throughout the witness of the early church and the Scriptures themselves, the Jesus message was something that was meant to be shared. The question in our day is, how do you share it well? Is there a way to do evangelism that isn't so, well you know, evangelism-y? Can we share our faith in a way that lets both the medium and message be good news? What would this kind of evangelism look like, and how would we do it? That is the question this chapter means to answer.[1]

Our Take...

The word *evangelism* comes from the Greek word *euangelion*, which means, simply, "good news, gospel, or evangel." Evangelism then is simply the work of "proclaiming the good news." Now, what you might not know is that *euangelion* is a term the church took from the empire that persecuted her during the first century. In an imperial sense, *euangelion* was a pronouncement from Rome's caesar. It was a declaration designed to remind the people of the empire who the king was and what he was up to. When the church takes up this word to describe what God is doing in Jesus, she does so with great intentionality. She is challenging the authority and story of the empire by making a counter claim about, first, who the true King is, and second, what the King is doing. Let's look at each in turn.

One of the ways Caesar's rule was affirmed during the first century AD was with the phrase "Caesar is Lord." Those who proclaimed that "Caesar is Lord" acknowledged their place as subjects of the empire's rule and affirmed its authority in their lives. Knowing this, the church began to use the phrase "Jesus is Lord"[2] in her letters and liturgies. In so doing, she was announcing that all other would-be kings and self-styled dictators are not top dog and that their days are numbered. The church was proclaiming that Jesus, and Jesus alone, is King.

Furthermore, by proclaiming that the kingdom of God has come, the church was telling a different story about what the true King is up to. The caesar of Rome was offering "salvation"[3] to the world through conquest and domination. According to the caesar, his dominion was God's gift to the people, and if they resisted, a public spectacle would be made of them as they were tortured on a cross. The church's version of events was very different. For the church, salvation came not from a fear of the cross but because of it. As Jesus was dominated by the empire unto death on the cross, He was acting to set everything right and inaugurate a new creation right in the middle of our current one. This is a radically alternative story about what the true King was doing. For the church, King Jesus was healing the world, not dominating it. God was fixing everything that is wrong and Jesus' resurrected body was the first marker of that renewed,[4] healed,[5] and restored[6] creation. For the church, evangelism is the announcement that, in spite of what things may look like, God really is making all things new.[7]

These two examples point to an important reality when it comes to evangelism in our day. Because evangelism is first and foremost an announcement about what the real story of creation is and who is in charge, when we think of what it should look like, we must let go of the idea that we have to convert anyone. Conversion is God's job, not ours. Conversion is about change at the deepest levels of a person. By some definitions, it is even the transformation of one substance into another. These are not things we can accomplish—but God can. Our misguided obsession with conversion has led us to try and insert ourselves into places of the human heart meant only for God. There's a word for this—idolatry. The good news (pun intended) is that this is easy to avoid since evangelism as we are called to doesn't involve converting anyone; it only involves announcing God's good news.

An example of this is the story in the book of Acts when Jewish Peter goes to the house of Cornelius, the Gentile. Although these two people could not be together by Jewish law, God's Spirit prompted Cornelius to send for Peter. When Peter arrived at the house, he was able to see what God was doing and connected the dots between Cornelius's experience and the story of Jesus. "Peter's friends from Joppa—all of them Jewish, all circumcised—were stunned to see that the gift of the Holy Spirit was poured out even on outsiders" (Acts 10:45–46). Here was an example of God moving in the people and changing them; Peter simply announced what he saw God already doing. This sharing of the news is evangelism; it is the announcement that God is healing the world and that Jesus is King! Will this sometimes require sacrifice? Yes. Can it be dangerous like it was for those early Christians? Absolutely. Does a gospel announcement demand choice? Certainly. However, it is in the act of announcing these things in any of the thousands of ways we can, that evangelism occurs. No attempt at conversion is necessary.

Evangelism Without Words

I was interviewing two college students for this chapter and one of them said to me,

> The thing Christians need to understand is that, for non-Christians, the whole "street-evangelism" thing is a joke. It's offensive and it also just doesn't work. It's not like I came into Christian faith because a stranger walked up to me and gave me this piece of information I didn't know and I was like, "Wow! Okay, I'm in." That's not how it works. I came to faith

because a group of Christians showed me with their lives what it meant to follow Jesus and demonstrated that love to me. That's what made it compelling (not the information but the action).

The gospel is true, and it is a truth that is first and foremost embodied. Evangelism is an announcement that Jesus is King and that announcement begins with how we live our lives. What does God's kingdom look like? See the way I'm living and you'll know.[8] This is one of the reasons the confession booth scene in the *Blue Like Jazz* movie is so compelling. Don has just been made the pope and his first act of "ministry" is to hear the outgoing pope's confession. However, before the former pope of Reed College can begin speaking, Don jumps in and confesses how *he* has misrepresented God. He apologizes for all the ways he has made God look bad through his choices and relationships. The former pope is stunned and forgives Don. This is a profoundly evangelistic moment because what Don understands is that the message of Jesus' kingship is not information that is disseminated—it is truth that is embodied. The Word was made flesh and dwelt among us after all.[9] That's why it's our job to make Jesus the living Word fleshed out in every part of our own lives. What would it look like if God were really running the show around here? This is why I love the fact that Don has become pope before this moment of realization.

In Roman Catholic theology, the pope is the chief pastor of the church and the Vicar of Christ on the earth. The pope's role is pastoral (he cares for the spiritual well-being of the people), but it's also sacramental. He points toward something far greater than himself because he is expected to speak and act for God. When Don becomes pope, it's as though he really understands this for the first time. He realizes that everything he does actually matters because his actions point toward something bigger—God. In this way, we are all called to see ourselves as little popes because everything we do matters in the same way. We proclaim what God is like with our lives.

Which brings me to one of the anxieties I hear voiced most about doing evangelism: "I just don't know what to say." I understand this anxiety, but it misses the point. The first question in evangelism is not "What should I say about God when I'm asked?"; it's "What am I already saying?" You are already saying something about God with the way to talk to the cashier at the grocery store, smile at a stranger in an elevator, or choose to call your mother on her birthday. This is why the Scriptures say, "What you experienced in the good news we brought you was more than words channeling down your ears; it came to you as a life-empowering, Spirit-infused message that offers complete hope and assurance!"[10] The gospel is more than words. It is also the action of God's people announcing God's new world order with even the most mundane details of their lives. In this way, we evangelize loudly, but without words.

Evangelism with Words

St. Francis is famously quoted as saying, "Preach the gospel at all times and when necessary use words." I love this quote because it challenges Christians to examine their lives as vehicles for evangelism. However, on one occasion, when he was invited to meet a Muslim sultan who found his lifestyle deeply compelling, Francis indeed used words when he preached to the ruler.[11] Eventually, words will come into play as we share the good news. So, how do we do that well?

First, remember that in evangelism, our words answer questions.

When my children were younger, they were dependent on my wife and me for everything, including understanding their very unique language. Before my son could talk, he would point to a cup with his juice in it and grunt. Noticing that he wanted the cup, my wife and I would connect the object with its proper name: "Cup. That's a cup." This happened over and over again until he learned that the blue plastic object with the screw-top lid is a "cup." Not long after his first birthday, I realized we were doing the same thing for the word *love*. I had told him I loved him numerous times but it was only when he got older that he was able to connect the word *love* with all the ways we had demonstrated it (food, drink, hugs, discipline, smiles, songs, play) over the years.

This is exactly how our words work when it comes to evangelism. Our words give context and explanation to our actions. When our lives are lived in a way that demonstrate the good news, people notice and ask. These conversations about Jesus and our motivations to live His teachings flow naturally. They are not forced or confrontational because they were asked for. Now is a good point to remember Jesus' admonition about all this in Matthew's gospel. When speaking to the disciples about their ministry, He told them, "Don't worry about what to say or how to say it. The words you should speak will be given to you. For at that moment, it will not be you speaking; it will be the Spirit of your Father speaking through you" (10:19–20). Jesus was referencing what would happen if and when the disciples were arrested. If they could trust God for the right words when they were facing imprisonment and death, how much more can we trust Him when we are asked to give content to the actions of our faith? Our words in evangelism come first to answer questions, and then we trust the Spirit for how we'll respond.[12]

Second, words tell your story.

We live in a culture where people see more than forty thousand advertising images a day[13], so people are very sensitive to having products and ideas sold to them. When it comes to using words in evangelism, remember that you are not selling anything, so be careful of words and phrases that sound like you are pitching a product. Evangelism is about proclamation, not marketing. Announcing, not pitching. In evangelism, we are not salesmen, but instead truth-tellers. This involves speaking frankly about what God has done in your life and your heart. It means sharing that there are different ways to live and expressing your conviction that things can actually change.

Another dynamic of this truth telling involves admitting that you are a Christian in the first place. It is who you are, a true part of yourself. Your faith is something authentic about your life, and that's a good thing. You don't need to be ashamed of that. In fact, to hide this part of who you are is to tell a lie. You are willfully concealing part of who you are and what you value as a person. That's not good for anybody. Tell the truth by sharing this part of yourself when you are asked. I know this can feel threatening, but consider the story one college student told me:

> I was dating a guy for a while and he knew I was a Christian. It didn't come up all the time because he was not into faith, but one night we were talking about our beliefs and he asked me about it. I had just listened to him talk about his belief system and how he doesn't believe in God, but when I told him that I did believe he started arguing with me. I was really taken aback as he began to debate me: "You can never prove that God is real. How can you be smart about most things

but believe in these fairy tales?" But before he could really get going, I just stopped him and said, "Wait! I just listened to you tell me about your beliefs without judgment because I want to know you. Now you are debating me when I'm doing the same? That's not fair. This is not the conversation we are having. I am sharing about myself with you and you are not allowed to debate me about that." After I said this he realized what he had done and instantly started apologizing. Because I had listened to him and then shared my story, it turned the tables on all the way he wanted to turn Christianity into a big fight. No one can argue with your story.

Using our words in evangelism can be as simple as telling the truth and sharing your story.

Third, words know when to keep quiet.

We often think of evangelism as speaking, but sometimes simply listening to others' stories and experiences can be evangelistic in its own rite. I have a friend who works for a Christian college that hired a Muslim faculty member a few years ago. Over the school year, this faculty member attended all the required chapel services and observed each Christian holiday on campus, however, when he requested the use of the school's chapel for Jumu'ah Prayers on Fridays, people wondered if it might cause a scandal. The dean of the college, compelled by the values of Christian hospitality, as outlined in the Rue of St. Benedict, granted him the request; and from then on, each Friday morning, the chapel was reconfigured for Jumu'ah then put back together for Christian worship Sunday morning. Later that year at a faculty meeting, the professor publicly thanked the dean and his colleagues for listening to his story and caring for his needs. He told them that he understood so much more about Jesus and what it meant to be a Christian by the way those Jesus followers made space for him to be a Muslim.

It kind of hurts your head, doesn't it? But it's true. Evangelism is not about conversion or marketing, but about showing others the love of God. It is the good news announcement that Jesus is King. It is making all things new when we listen, live with integrity, and tell our stories. It is a living announcement that is the heartbeat of true evangelism and that something each of us can do at all times, using words when necessary. Remember that the Holy Spirit will give you the vocabulary when you can't find it on your own, so trust God, and your faith will spread more easily than you think.

THE WAY IN . . .

Watch the scene during Renn Fayre between Don and the pope, followed by Don's DVD clip on evangelism.

1. What are your first associations with the word *evangelism*? Are they positive or negative?

2. Have you ever been evangelized? What was that like?

3. Don suggests that evangelism is about sharing our lives with others. Do you agree?

4. What makes evangelism hardest in our culture?

5. Is there anything that makes it easy?

EXPLORING FURTHER . . .

1. Did you learn something new in this chapter that you didn't know before? If so, what was it?

2. Who was the first person to share Jesus with you? How did they do it?

3. The author separates the announcement part of evangelism from conversion. Do you agree with this separation? What place does conversion have in evangelism?

4. Does it feel liberating or terrifying to consider that our actions proclaim things about God?

5. Has there ever been a time where you have evangelized by keeping quiet? If so, when? If not, what about the other two suggestions the author makes for using words in evangelism? Have you ever used those?

6. Is evangelism hard or easy for you? Why?

7. Share a story about a time when you evangelized or were evangelized well or poorly. What made it helpful or unhelpful?

CRAFTING YOUR RULE

1. Write down your faith story. Start at the beginning and mark five to ten major events that have affected you along the way. Include who shared the faith with you the first time and any ways God has worked in your life to change things.

2. How might someone respond if evangelized poorly?

3. How do you imagine responding if someone picks a fight with you over your faith?

4. What scares you the most about the prospect of evangelizing?

5. Who is the community that you are "putting flesh on the good news" with? What do you all "say" about God with your life together?

CHAPTER 8

GENDER

I want to start this chapter with a story I would use whether this book was connected to the *Blue Like Jazz* movie or not. The story focuses on Don's first meeting with Lauryn, which brings the topic of gender center-stage.

Don has just moved into his dorm at Reed College. His evangelical Baptist upbringing makes him feel at every turn like the consummate fish out of water. Needing to use the restroom, he heads down to the hall washroom and settles in at the urinal. Within moments he hears voices behind him and is shocked to see two women, who Don later finds out to be lesbians, walking into the bathroom. As Don moves quickly to conceal himself, it's obvious they couldn't care less. They are deep in a conversation about the relevance of Tori Amos, and without taking a break from their conversation, one of them, Lauryn, sidles up to the urinal next to Don to do her business. Don is wide-eyed through the whole thing, which makes the perfunctory nod she gives him as she crosses to the sink to wash her hands hilarious. It's just another day in the washroom at Reed College for her, but for Don it's yet another sign that he is not in Texas anymore.

I love this scene, not just for the way it introduces one of the film's main characters, but also for the way it demands a conversation about gender. What does it mean to be male and female anyway? Which parts of our gender identities are socially constructed, and which ones are not? How much of gender has to do with genitalia, and how much doesn't? If it's not confined to our "plumbing," then what measures do we use? These are conversations we rarely have these days, but they are important if we are going to figure out what it means to live as human beings made in God's image. This chapter will not give many definitive answers but will instead set you on a path toward asking better questions about how we might follow Jesus as a gendered being.

Our Take...

In May 2011, two Canadian parents made international news when word got out that they were raising their baby, Storm, as a genderless person.[1] What this meant was that no one, except for a few close relatives, was allowed to know Storm's sex. The parents, as the stories reported it, wanted the baby to "choose its gender" in order that she or he might be free from the cultural pressures of gender placed on children at even the youngest of ages. What these parents are calling into question is the way that cultural stereotypes influence our gender identities. Even as babies, girls are dressed in pink while boys are dressed in blue. Boys are given little trucks and dinosaurs to play with, while girls are given baby dolls and ponies. The goal in not revealing Storm's gender, even to Storm, is to challenge these stereotypes. Who says girls can't like trucks and boys can't like ponies? Who says boys can't wear pink, and girls can't wear blue? These constructions of gender are indeed built by the culture that each child is raised in. They affect each child's self-identity and even their definitions about what it means to be a man or a woman. Such realities drove Storm's parents to try and raise him or her free from gender constraints, which was hailed as brave by supporters and condemned as damaging by detractors.

What this story reminds me of is how little we really know about gender, and how bad we are at talking about it as a culture. Especially as a culture of Christians.

Jesus and Gender: Male and Female God Created Them

Any Christian conversation about gender has to start with Genesis 1:27: "So God did just that. He created humanity in His image, created them male and female." When God created the first humans, He made both a man and a woman. This gender distinction of male and female was part of God's good creation, before sin and death entered the picture. It was a good part of the good creation.

Furthermore, Adam and Eve's vocation to image God in the creation had gender tied to it. Remember when God said, "It is not good for the man to be alone."[2] This comes in relation to Adam's instruction to care for and work in the garden. The creation project requires women and men to do the God imaging together. It is not sufficient for either to go it alone. Because of this, we should see our genders as gifts. They are part of the good creation, and as such, they act as a marker pointing toward the way things are supposed to be.

Now, most conversations we have about gender today collapse into one of two mistakes. The first is the adoption of cultural stereotypes for our definitions of male and female. What I'm talking about are those stereotypes that say men are supposed to be tough, in control, emotionless, and self-sufficient; while women are supposed to be sensitive, empathetic, nurturing, and passive. Have you ever heard phrases like "Be a man!" or "Grow a pair" or "Stop mothering me"? They come from these stereotypes. If you have ever run across these stereotypes or felt pressured to fit into them, you're not alone. There is a lot of pressure to fit our masculinity or femininity into these categories.

However, in the kingdom of God, there is no one-size-fits-all box when it comes to gender. There are plenty of women who are self-sufficient and analytical, and plenty of men who are nurturing and sensitive. To force all of masculinity into one box and all of femininity into another defaces the goodness of our God-made genders. Masculine and feminine are far more complicated and nuanced categories than any stereotype will allow, which is why part of following Jesus in our genders means letting go of the stereotypes.

The second mistake we make in talking about gender is claiming that gender does not exist or that it is simply a false distinction. This position sometimes comes in response to the darker and more destructive side to the adoption of cultural stereotypes. That is, when one gender is privileged over or allowed to abuse another. When gender stereotypes are used to create and justify hierarchies in which one gender dominates, represses, or tyrannizes another in the name of God's creative design,[3] it should be called what it is—sin. Gender should never be used to subjugate, oppress, or abuse another person.

Ever.

Period.

In the name of Jesus.

However, our response to these constrictive stereotypes should not be to claim that gender is a false distinction by asserting that there is no difference between male and female. It is true that gender should not be a limitation or liability when it comes to getting a job or procuring the rites of citizenship. However, attempting to gain societal equality by saying that gender simply doesn't matter takes it too far.

This is because our masculinity and femininity are part of God's good creation. They are markers of the way things are supposed to be. They are also part of the way things will be again in the new heaven and new earth. Our resurrected bodies will have gender. So we can't call for equity and justice between men and women by pretending our genders don't exist. This disrespects both and redeems neither. We have to live in a way that brings out the "goodness" in both genders if we are to work with God in making the kingdom come on earth as it is in heaven.

You Can't See What You Can't See

In 2005, I took a group of students to Mississippi to do cleanup after Hurricane Katrina. On the way home, we stopped in Memphis, Tennessee, and because we were staying downtown, we had dinner on the world-famous Beale Street. Beale Street is a tourist destination during the day, but after about 8:00 pm they barricade the ends of the street and the whole block becomes one big club. There are live bands playing everywhere and lots of folks out dancing and having a good time. I planned to lead my group through a prayer exercise where they would "seek the kingdom on Beale Street." So I sorted them all into small groups, put each with a leader, and sent them all out for an hour or so. Their task was to walk around and see what evidence of God's kingdom they could find amidst the party goers.

When the hour was up, I gathered us all in a park to share. I expected to hear stories about the beauty of music or how we shouldn't judge a book by its cover. What I got instead caught me totally off guard. One of the senior girls started crying, and through her tears told me that what stuck out the most to her were the women who had come downtown to party. She described the way they dressed in revealing clothing, how they flirted in highly sexual ways, and how the men responded with attention, affection, and affirmation. The way these women had begged men to sexualize them was obvious to my student, and she hated the whole thing . . . because of how jealous she was. She continued explaining that, as much as she knew it was dark and gross, she wanted to look like those women and get the attention they were getting. But at the same time she hated herself for wanting those things. Feeling utterly trapped, she could only cry.

However, it wasn't only this one student who felt like this. At that moment, nearly all the women on our trip spoke up indicating that they had similar experiences. As I tried to get a handle on what was happening, a sophomore girl added, "I think it was all just so obvious tonight, because we have been with you guys [referencing the men in the circle] all week and you never treat us like that."

I didn't quite know what to do next. As half of my girls choked back tears and my guys looked around like deer caught in headlights, I made the executive decision to take us all back to the hotel. Once there, all twenty-five of us piled into one room and for the next hour or so, we just listened to each other. The men listened to the women tell their stories about how they experience the misogyny that seems to be woven into the very fabric of our culture.[4] How they live in a "fear of being raped" dynamic that affects their very experience of safety on a daily basis. How advertising and other media compound the anxiety that drives eating disorders. But it wasn't just a one-way street. The women listened to the men describe their fears of being sexually humiliated in the locker room. About the ways they feel pressured by other men to treat women like objects and about how pornography ties into the whole thing. Together they sat, on the floor of a hotel room, sharing openly, and actively listening to one another's stories.

This "together" is a key component to moving forward in any sort of healthy understanding of gender. We didn't take the men into one room and the women into another to have this conversation, and it was the best choice I made all night. The togetherness meant that the guys could finally gain insight into the deep and daily struggles that plague females, and the girls could begin to understand that it's tough for guys too. Neither of the sexes had any idea what the other was going through.

And that is the point—none of us can know what it is like to be another gender in this culture until we engage one another in a dialogue. We just can't see what we can't see and that's why I ask, "What is it like to be a woman in this culture today?" Because as a man I have no idea unless a woman tells me.

This is where a Jesus-centered, redeemed conversation about gender must go. When we share our stories of pride and pain openly and freely with members of the opposite gender and they listen in love, it helps us see where the "God-made goodness" of our genders is being squashed out and gives us an opportunity to strategize how to redeem that. The redemption of our genders is tied up in each other's freedom. Like it was in the beginning, we have to work together to accomplish God's purposes.

That's what I learned that night in Memphis. You really can't see what you can't see. I had no idea what going out to Beale St. that night would evoke in our girls. No idea at all—because I'm not a woman. Everything I do, see, and understand is conditioned by the fact that I am a man. It just is. I can't avoid this fact and I shouldn't. It's good that I am a man. But I always need to remember that there is another perspective out there and that because of my maleness it may not be immediately apparent to me. I can't see it until somebody shows me; therefore, I need not be afraid to ask.

Beautiful Gender

I want to conclude this chapter with an admonition for all of us Christians regarding the way we think, act, and talk about gender. Gender is a tricky topic. There is a great deal of nuance to it and it is easier to say what it's *not* than what it *is* these days. I think that's okay. We are in the middle of a big shift in our understanding of what it means to be male and female in this culture and, even though it's a conversation with plenty of pitfalls, it's worth having. So, because the language around all this is so loaded and difficult to get precisely right, let's not try. Instead let's orient ourselves around trying to say something helpful about gender every time we discuss it and let us listen to each other with generosity, humility, and patience, so that our conversations turn out, well, beautiful. By this, I mean they are wonderful to look at and experience from the inside out. Christian conversations about gender should show what active listening, respectful inquiry, and humble assertions look like when a sensitive topic is on the table. What a change this will be from the ridiculous ranting of cable news and snarky blog posts. There are plenty of bad and hurtful conversations about gender out there; let's not have one of those. Let's instead ask questions about how we can make this conversation concerning gender beautiful. Then perhaps we will start to demonstrate how good our genders really are and show everybody in our culture how it's to be done.

THE WAY IN . . .

Re-read the description of Don's first encounter with Lauryn in the bathroom. (Clip of this scene is not available on DVD.)

1. What are your impressions of this interaction?

2. Why does Lauryn catch Don off guard in the bathroom?

3. How would this encounter have been different if the gender roles were reversed?

EXPLORING FURTHER . . .

1. What do you think about baby Storm? Did Storm's parents get it right or wrong?

2. What does it mean to be a man? What does it mean to be a woman? Are your answers to these questions truly sex specific?

3. How much of gender has to do with genitalia? How much does not?

4. Are there any gender roles you inherited? Where did they come from?

5. The author says Christians fall into two traps when we discuss gender in our culture—we baptize stereotypes or we say gender is irrelevant. Do you agree? Why or why not?

6. What would a beautiful conversation about gender look, sound, and feel like? Have you ever had one?

CRAFTING YOUR RULE

1. Finish this sentence: "I first knew I was a woman/man when . . ."

Why did you finish the sentence the way you did? How much does your answer have to do with gender?

2. Have you ever listened to someone else's story about being another gender? What was it like?

3. Who in your life can you have beautiful conversations about gender with?

4. Does anything scare you about conversations regarding gender?

5. What would help lessen that fear? Are there people you could talk to who would help the conversation turn beautiful?

CHAPTER 9

MONEY

Of all the markers of adulthood,[1] the one that remains tricky for many is financial independence. This is not simply because good jobs are hard to find but also because many emerging adults make financial choices in their early twenties that directly affect the rest of their lives. Now, at this point you might be thinking I'm going to launch into a tirade about credit cards and the dangers of their misuse. While that's worth mentioning, of equal importance is the way emerging adults approach student loans and the perspectives they have on saving, spending, and giving. So, with all this on the table I'd like to talk first about how God sees money, then suggest some basics for navigating the wild world of emerging adult financial management. Finally, I'll explore places where we may be commanded to spend a bit more than we think we should in pursuit of God's justice.

Our Take...

When I got my driver's license I had the privilege of driving myself to school. With that came the added responsibility of getting myself out of the house on time—something I was not good at.

One particular morning, I was running late because I couldn't find the pair of socks I wanted to wear. I had looked high and low and eventually found them in the washing machine—wet. Most normal people would just choose a different pair of socks at this point, but not my sixteen-year-old self. I started formulating a plan to dry the socks in a hurry. But what to use? The dryer? No, it would take too long. My mother's hair dryer? Same problem. Wear them wet? No, that would be weird. What to do? What to do? And then it hit me like a bolt of pure inspiration—the microwave! Yes, this will be perfect. It heats things up in no time flat. Genius! So, before I could stop and think about it I threw my damp socks in the microwave and set the timer for sixty seconds.

When I heard popping sounds from inside the device, I looked through the glass to see a bright yellow flame and white sparks erupting from my socks. "Ahhhhh!" I screamed, rushing over. I flung the door of the microwave open, but by that time it was too late. Both my socks and our microwave were destroyed. In a crude way, this illustrates how Christians are to approach and manage money.

Money is a tool. Not unlike a microwave oven, it enables work to get done. Money is what people use to buy and sell goods in order to meet their basic needs. By God's design, money is not inherently evil or against the Creator. Used rightly, money enables both human survival and prosperity as a means of getting people what they need.

However, like the microwave, if money is used for purposes other than what it was created for, it can be a destructive force. It can be used to destroy the creation both by its use and the way it's acquired. Money can even be used to keep others from getting what they need when some take more of it than they can ever spend, giving nothing to those who need it most. It can become the focus of a person's whole life instead of the love and service of God. Such misuses are why Jesus teaches, "People try to serve both God and money—but you can't."[2] Either you'll love God and hate money, or vice versa. Having allegiance to both won't work because when it comes to money, we have a choice: we can use it to bring heaven to earth—or we can use it for something else entirely.

God warned the Israelites of this kind of thing before they entered the land of Canaan. Yahweh had given the people the Torah in order to teach them how to live well with God. The Jews were God's chosen people and He had promised to care for them and provide everything they needed upon entering the promised land. However, God also knew that even a little prosperity could be a dangerous thing, so in Deuteronomy 8 the people of Israel were warned not to forget to honor the Torah.[3] Otherwise, when everything was going well for them, when they had eaten all they wanted and were satisfied, when their herds and flocks grew, when their bank accounts swelled, the people would become proud.

They would forget the God who gave them prosperity and take the credit for themselves. They would say, "I did this by my own strength and power—I pulled myself up by my own bootstraps here—so all of it belongs to me and I can do with it as I please." In response to this God warned, "Remember the Eternal One your God. He's the One who gives you the power to get wealth, so He can keep the covenant promises He made to your ancestors, as He is doing now."[4]

This whole passage is getting at the basic truth that everything belongs to God.[5] Everything. So, anything we possess, including our money, is a gift from God.[6] We are in charge of things that don't belong to us. Therefore, we have a responsibility to use and allocate these gifts in ways that please their owner. What Yahweh knew about people in Deuteronomy 8 is also true of us. When things are going well for us—when we've eaten all we want, when our jobs are going great, when we've got plenty of money—our temptation will be to forget who it all belongs to and believe it actually belongs to us. This, like wet socks in a microwave, will only lead to our ruin.

This is why the ancient Hebrews saw wealth as a burden. The more you had, the greater your responsibility to make sure it was handled properly. The assumption was that it mattered to God what you did with what you had been given and that everyone would one day be held accountable for the choices they had made.

This accountability to God's dream is what makes up the core of God's justice. It's God's big plan of setting right everything in the whole creation.[7] In Jesus, God is healing the creation and making everything as it is meant to be, so as humans, we are either part of the problem or part of the solution. This applies directly to our choices about money. It is a tool meant to bring heaven to earth because that is what its owner desires.

The Way of Money in Emerging Adulthood

Because this is a book about faith during emerging adulthood, I would like to offer some very pragmatic advice about how you relate to money. These are a few guidelines for how to start bringing heaven to earth with your cash.

Don't Buy What You Can't Afford

Thanks to the cultural waters of consumerism a guiding principle of money for many is: buy now, pay later.[8] Credit cards offer the simplest and easiest way to do this, which is why, as an emerging adult, you will be buried in invitations from banks to get one. With a credit card you can purchase whatever you need until you hit your credit limit. You pay for everything with the card, the credit card company agrees to cover the costs, and then you reimburse them when your bill comes at the end of each month. However, if you can't pay everything off in one month it's no problem. The credit card company is still happy to cover your costs until you can pay it all back; all you have to do is pay a fee. That fee, or interest, is calculated based on a percentage of the amount you owe. This arrangement is how the credit card company makes its money.[9]

The problem comes when credit cards are used to buy more than the purchaser can afford. The purchaser then ends up carrying a huge amount of debt that grows and grows because the interest they owe continues to build each month as well. Many EAs incorrectly assume that they are paying down their debt when they make the minimum monthly payment on their statement. In reality, by paying the minimum they are only paying off a small percentage of the total interest they owe and haven't touched what's called the principle.[10] This means that the next month the purchaser owes the credit card company the principle plus the interest that wasn't paid the month before in addition to the new interest on that total amount of debt. It can be a vicious and enslaving cycle, but can be avoided if you buy only what you can afford.[11]

This same value needs to be applied to student loans. In 2010, student loans overshadowed credit cards as the largest debt burden on American pocketbooks.[12] Many EAs pay for college by taking out massive loans without giving any thought to how they will pay those loans back—until it's too late. Even students who have frugal spending habits don't apply those habits to student loans. The conventional wisdom is, when it comes to education, you should agree to pay whatever it takes to get the best degree you can, even if it means taking out massive loans. Nothing could be further from the truth. What's worse is the increasing number of stories about parents taking out loans in their children's names only to get in over their heads, and leave the child saddled with the debt themselves.

So, be an active participant in every part of your financial decision-making process. You will be responsible for paying back any loans you take out (or that are taken out in your name), and the money you have to do that with will come from the job you land after college. So, anyone contemplating student loans needs to consider whether or not the starting salary for jobs in your field of choice will allow you to pay all your bills after graduation— including student loans. A good rule of thumb is not to take out more money over your four years of undergraduate education than you can make in your first year of employment. So, if the starting salary for a nurse is between $40,000 and $45,000 in your region, it would be fine to borrow up to $10,000 a year to pay for a four-year education that helps you get that job. However, if you are taking out loans in the six figures to fund a degree where the starting salary is $25,000–$30,000, then you have essentially bought a degree you cannot afford.

I am not trying to persuade you from "following your dreams."[13] What I am trying to say is that these days you have to think about how to make money off of your degree before you agree to pay for it. That way, if you want to study the old standby example of blow-off degrees (such as underwater basket weaving), you can make sure to do it at a less-expensive school because your employment opportunities after graduation are going to be limited.

Live on a Budget

Bringing it back to the day-to-day good stewardship, don't forget to live on a budget. A budget is just a simple breakdown that compares all your monthly expenses (rent, food, bills, debt, charity, entertainment, savings, etc.) to your monthly income. Take stock of everything you are spending in one month; and if it is equal to or less than what you are bringing in, then you are golden. This budget should include some sort of giving to the church, often called a tithe. Tithing reminds us who our money belongs to, where it comes from, and how it is supposed to be used. One doesn't need to give much;[14] it is the act of tithing that is important in our lives.

This type of accounting is easy for certain personality types. They love to get into the details and minutiae of their financial choices with the latest budgeting software and smart phone apps. However, there are others of us (and I count myself among them) for whom looking at our expenses just makes us tired. We have little energy for such detail and are often afraid of what we might find. Unfortunately, this is the point where folks like us have to just suck it up. Living on a balanced budget is part of our responsibility to godly stewardship. It's certainly not the only thing, but it's a part of it.[15]

Give a Little Bit

One of the inescapable elements of Jesus' teaching is to be generous with what you have.[16] Because all of our money belongs to God and we have a responsibility to make sure that it goes where God wants it to be, we should expect to be generous givers with our resources. In the Old Testament, the Israelites were to follow the Torah's teaching that 10 percent of everything they had be used to help the needy who worked in the temple.[17] This is a fine place to start, but Jesus took it a step farther by asking for a deeper kind of generosity.[18] His earliest followers embodied His teaching by considering the needs of the poor their own responsibility, even giving up their own possessions to care for them.[19] So, it's not as if we should just give 10 percent to God and assume that the rest belongs to us. *All* of it belongs to God first, so the question to ask about our money is, "God, where do You want all this to end up?" From here we operate out of a place of trust that God will care for us as much as we care for others.[20]

Save a Little Bit

Last but not least, keep an eye on your future as you enter financial independence. Saving can be a helpful part of stewardship. However, while there are lots of ways to save money for the things you might need in the future (retirement, graduate school, your children's education), keep two things in mind. First, save justly. Jesus pointed out that what matters most when giving is not the size of a gift but that God's justice is being done.[21] This applies to savings as well. Pay attention to where you put your money. Ask important questions. Are the investments being made on your behalf ethical? Is your money going to companies and interests that are counter to God's kingdom? Saving justly may mean choosing less-profitable accounts, but that is okay. It's God we trust for our future and provision anyway, not our bank accounts.

Second, save with an eye on the present. In keeping with the value of God's justice, remember that there may be real needs around *now* that are more worthy than your possible needs *later.* So if you have a friend and she needs help getting her child a doctor's appointment, good stewardship might dictate that you hold out for a month on your savings plan so you can help pay for that visit. When weighing present needs against possible future needs, remember that in God's kingdom there is always enough.

Consider the High Cost of Low Prices

It is possible to buy many things in the United States, like food, clothing, and housewares, at phenomenally low prices. Prices our forbearers could never have dreamed of. However, sometimes what makes those low prices possible are wildly unjust labor and production practices that exploit people in other countries and seriously damage everyone's natural resources. As much as living within your means and on a budget makes good sense, it doesn't mean that chasing the best deal all the time is always the right thing to do. In fact, Christian practice may demand just the opposite.

A while ago, my wife and I became aware that the fruits and vegetables we bought so inexpensively at the supermarket down the street had some hidden costs—namely the large amounts of energy and pollutants being used to process and transport these foods when they were not in season.[22] When we started to make these connections, we did some research and ultimately joined a local CSA, or Community Supported Agriculture. With a CSA we buy a share of a local farm's produce and the farmer provides us with a box every week with the fruits and vegetables they grow. We are members of both a summer and a winter CSA, and these have helped us eat more reasonably and seasonably. The thing is, our CSA costs more than if we bought our vegetables at the supermarket every week. It has required sacrifice in other areas, but it has been worth it for us. Not because we get to feel "more right" about our food choices, but because we experience our CSA choice as a way of using our money as part of the solution. Although it might not be possible for all of us to join a CSA, farmers markets are generally accessible. Making a trip to the farmers market can be a fun weekend activity, and allows you to support local farmers instead of the factory farming industry whose practices can be unethical.

I'll bet you've got stories of your own. Stories of people not doing what's cheap so they can do what's right. What is your story going to be?[23] Our money is a tool that can be part of the problem or part of God's solution. It just depends on how it's handled. So how are you going to handle it?

THE WAY IN . . .

Watch Don's DVD clip on money.

I. What do you think about Don's comment that being poor in the United States means having more money than much of the rest of the world?

2. Is it fair that this is the case? Why or why not?

3. Does this economic imbalance require something different of Christians living in the United States than in other parts of the world?

4. What is the role of governments in economic justice?

5. What is the role of the church in economic justice?

6. What organizations do you know that are already working to bring justice?

EXPLORING FURTHER . . .

1. Have you ever seen money bring heaven to earth by the way it was used? Explain.

2. Have you ever seen money bring hell to earth by the way it was used? Explain.

3. The author argues that our money doesn't belong to us but instead belongs to God. Do you agree with this? Why or why not?

4. Give examples where you have seen giving and saving done "justly."

5. Check out the endnotes at the end of the book. In endnote 23, the author lists three Christian organizations working for economic justice. Go online and explore what one of these groups is doing to make God's kingdom come in regard to money.

CRAFTING YOUR RULE

1. How were you taught to handle money? Who taught you? Has that instruction been helpful?

2. Are you ever tempted to buy more than you can afford? Where and when?

3. Where and how much do you give away? Are there any areas in which you are tempted to hold back? Why do you think that is? Read Jesus' commentary about giving in Mark 12:41–44. Does this teaching challenge or comfort you?

4. How can you take the first step toward saving?

5. Where might you be called to spend more because of God's justice?

6. Who will you talk to about your choices?

PARTYING

I'll never forget the first time I saw the movie *Animal House*.
I was in college and, there, in the student union of my university,
I was introduced to Faber College, the antics of Delta house, and
Otis Day and the Nights. The occasion is memorable because
when the movie ended, I thought, *Wow! My college experience isn't
anything like that. Am I doing this right?* Now, without going too far
down a "which came first—the chicken or the egg?" rabbit trail,
Animal House and all the films that imitate it make up sort of a
feedback loop for what college life is "supposed to be." There is a
perception that college life will include crazy parties (cue the toga
chants) and that this partying must include large amounts of alcohol.
And even though statistically this is not far off, I wonder if this is the
way that college parties have to be.

From a numbers standpoint, if you're going to college, you're
probably going to end up at parties where alcohol is being served.
Over 84 percent of emerging adults ages eighteen to twenty-two
say that they have consumed alcohol in the last year, with over 46
percent admitting to binge drinking during that same time frame.[1]
However, even with these kinds of facts on the table, the *perception*
of alcohol use is even more staggering. A staggering 91 percent of

students polled *believe* that their peers are drinking at least once a week (whether or not they actually are) and 52 percent believe the same is true for illegal drugs.[2] Statistics like these show why there is a powerful pressure to drink alcohol while socializing in college, because as far as anyone knows, *everyone* is doing it.[3]

The question this raises for me is not, "How do we combat underage drinking?" or "How can we avoid parties altogether?" but instead, "What would God-blessed partying look like?"

Parties are not bad . . . in fact, I think they're pretty good. We must understand, however, that celebrating in a way that is redemptive will require some intentionality. Would alcohol be involved at God-blessed parties? What kinds of things would people do at God-blessed parties? What wouldn't they do? Since the parties that get all the airtime (like the ones in *Animal House* or bad reality shows) seem to dehumanize people, how can we celebrate in ways that re-humanize them? How can we party in a way that glorifies God?

Our Take . . .

I was in a band in high school and we played a lot of gigs at parties thrown by my classmates. We were rarely paid for any of these gigs, because we played for free beer—and lots of it. When I got serious about my faith (just before my senior year), one of the first inconsistencies I noticed in myself was how much I drank. Not only was I underage, but I was also drinking in order to get drunk. Plain and simple, drunkenness was my goal. All this left me conflicted about parties because, in my experience, they were a place where out-of-control things happened. What if drinking alcohol, and partying in general, were just plain wrong? Fortunately, in reading the Bible, I was set straight.

All through the Bible, parties are not just tolerated; they are commanded. God told Israel to arrange her life around seven big parties[4] every year. These parties were to take place on a fixed cycle, and together they told the story of Israel's rescue from slavery in Egypt. Some of them were connected to the harvest (which means they celebrated the end of hard labor), and one in particular (the Passover) required (that's right, required!) participants to drink four glasses of wine. So, partying in the Old Testament was a theological activity. Their parties said things about God.

In the New Testament, the party continued. Jesus participated in all of the feasts mentioned above during His life, attended at least one scandalous dinner party,[5] and helped out at a wedding that famously ran short of wine.[6] He even used party imagery to paint pictures of what God's right-side-up world looks like.[7] Over and over again, the Bible reminds us that parties are not things that draw us from the love of God; how we participate in them is where the problem lies.

Party On...

Okay, okay. I get it. Partying is part of the Christian life. So what do these God-honoring parties look like? Well, I'm glad you asked. Here are a few parameters . . .

Party on Purpose

Good and God-blessed parties celebrate legitimate accomplishments. If you ask the average college-aged partygoer why they are celebrating, many won't have an answer (or they'll pick something senseless—"It's Friday!"). The problem with "pointless partying" is that it quickly becomes an excuse to overindulge. Don't go there. Like those harvest festivals in the Old Testament, celebrate the significant accomplishments of life: graduations, marriages, births, the completion of hard work, and even deaths. These are all great reasons to get friends together and have a blast, even if you are mourning a great loss.

Party with People, not Just Near Them

Did you see Pixar's 2008 movie *Wall-E*? It's a great film about a robot who was left behind to clean up the earth after humans had trashed the planet so much they had to evacuate. If that set-up isn't challenging enough, things get really uncomfortable when Wall-E ends up onboard a spaceship only to find that all human beings are now morbidly obese and so utterly dependent on technology that they don't even walk anymore—they just glide around on floating chairs. In one scene, two people sit next to each other having what looks like a video chat–style conversation with other people. However, it's not long before the audience realizes that these two people are actually talking to each other! Even though they are sitting right next to one another and won't look each other in the face. They have to use the TV screens attached to their chairs instead. These humans have lost the ability to relate in person.

Are wild parties and "keggers" not an example of this same phenomenon? At these parties, a whole bunch of people stand around together, but drink so much that they never really relate to anyone in a meaningful way. Some have suggested this happens to EAs because they are trying to cope with their anxiety, and partying becomes a means of escape.[8] Whatever the reason, it is not an example of healthy partying at all. Good parties will help guests to cultivate relationships instead of evading them, because at God-blessed parties, people party with each other and not just near one another.

Party with Your Grandma!

Parties that look like God's right-side-up world will be intergenerational affairs. When Israel did her festival cycle, entire families were present and involved from the youngest child to the oldest adult. Parties that make us more human will include, at least occasionally, people from generations other than your own.

My wife and I are part of a monthly supper club that is made up of six different couples from four different generations. Our dinners together have been extremely enriching, because when you're talking to people who have been married longer than you've been alive, you are given a broader perspective on life and what matters most. I've heard it said that you need at least three generations present before an authentic community can exist. I can't verify where that statistic comes from, but it certainly feels true given my experience. So, whether it's with your own grandmother or someone else's, try to throw a few parties that are intergenerational. I'll bet it deepens the way you celebrate.

Party Like It's the End of the World

When I lived in Pittsburgh, some friends of mine planted a church among the homeless downtown. The church met on Sunday nights and invited youth groups like ours to provide dinner after the worship service. It was a great opportunity to serve, and they seemed to have no trouble lining up volunteers for every Sunday night of the year except one—Super Bowl Sunday.

When our youth group heard this, we made a decision. Let's take the money we would spend on our own Super Bowl party and use it to throw a *better* party for the members of this church. So, on Super Bowl Sunday, we showed up with a giant party sub, fresh fruit, veggies, dip, cookies, and some killer lemonade; and then, after worship, set up an old TV (complete with rabbit ears) and ate dinner together watching the big game.

During dinner I noticed that two of my junior high boys were sitting among some pretty haggard-looking older men. Although I didn't want to be overprotective, I kept an eye on them to make sure everyone was getting along well and that my boys were not being inappropriate. Suddenly, while I was watching them, there was a big play in the game and all of them started high-fiving each other as if they were in someone's living room. Homeless guys and thirteen-year-old boys—just hanging out and watching football like it was no big deal. Watching this transpire, I was struck by what a picture it was of God's redemption.

When we encounter the homeless it often makes us uncomfortable. We don't know how to act and make assumptions about what put them on the street in the first place. As a result, homeless men and women stop being treated like actual human beings. Instead they are seen as some kind of cultural garbage littering the streets. Furthermore, it is the teenagers in many cities who abuse them the most.[9] This dynamic drives many homeless people to not only avoid public places but actually act rudely toward youth they see on the street. Yet, here at this party these two groups of people were enjoying each other. They were sharing in a common celebration and the party provided the context for potential healing. Now, while I don't know everything about the particular stories of the homeless men that night and I'm sure my students have not been abusing them, their mutual celebration was a picture of how things are supposed to be in a kingdom where the divisions of the upside-down world are no more. That party affirmed to me that God really is healing things and, while we're not all the way there yet, moments like that (when thirteen-year-old boys and homeless men enjoy a game together) are a glimpse of where everything is headed.

In this way, that Super Bowl party gave me a glimpse of the end of the world. The end of the world—when God's work of redemption has been completed, heaven and earth are reunited, and everything is as it should be. The end of the world—when Jesus is worshipped by everybody, and sin and death are fully and finally defeated. The end of the world—a time that is so good and glorious the Scriptures say even the creation itself will rejoice when it arrives.[10] This is what I got a glimpse of at the party that night and it's made me wonder, what if all our parties looked like an end-of-the-world party? What if the question at the heart of Christian partying is about how we can bring heaven to earth with our celebrations? How would that affect the way we throw parties? Would it affect the way we celebrate at parties?

Partying Smart

I have a friend named John who is a personal trainer and works at a fitness facility near my house. He trains everyone from country music stars to average Joes and loves his job because he gets to see people enjoy the benefits of fitness like increased health, improved mood, and a sense of personal accomplishment. However, he often sees people come into his facility to exercise with little or no planning as to how they will do it. You can tell who they are because they will walk up to a piece of equipment, select the heaviest weight they can imagine, and then try to lift it by any means necessary. This approach usually results in injury and discouragement and has put some off exercise forever. John sees all this as completely unnecessary.

"Dixon, the key to this whole thing," he once told me, "is to train smart and not hard. Training hard means approaching your workout with nothing but intensity. However, this can leave you injured and missing the long-term benefits of exercise. Training smart, however, means doing a little planning before you hit the gym. It involves simple strategies like learning the form of an exercise before you attempt it, knowing your limits, and setting attainable goals. People that train smart stay more injury free and develop habits that can sustain a lifetime of fitness."

What if partying is the same way? What if Christians are supposed to party smart and not hard? Hard partying can be fun by certain standards, but over time it is unsustainable. Like those folks who come into the gym cold, trying to bench-press their body weight, partying hard can leave us injured, discouraged, and broken. Partying smart, however, can produce different results. Like with those who have a plan going into the gym, partying smart can bring health, enjoyment, and satisfaction because there is more to celebration than just intensity.

May the suggestions in this chapter be a starting place for all of us to party smart.

Celebration is part of God's right-side-up world, but to do it right requires a little planning. What will your plan be? Who will you ask to join you in it? Who could train you in healthy partying? As we answer these questions, our revelry may indeed become revelation and we may hear the voice of the Spirit urging us to party on!

THE WAY IN . . .

Watch the Renn Fayre party scene from the movie, followed by Don's DVD clip on parties.

1. What is your reaction to the partying taking place in the movie?

2. Does it look similar to your experiences? Why or why not?

3. Why do you think people party like this?

4. What aspects of Renn Fayre look like God-blessed partying?

5. What aspects of Renn Fayre do not? How can you tell the difference?

EXPLORING FURTHER . . .

1. What is the best party you can remember going to? What was it like? What made it "the best"?

2. Is there something you celebrate every year? What is it and who do you like to celebrate with?

3. Do you agree with the author's contention that partying is a theological activity? Why or why not?

4. What kind of partying do you normally engage in?

5. What are good boundaries for your parties?

6. Is it ever okay to party without a reason? Why or why not?

7. Do you agree with the author's metaphor that partying is like exercising?

8. What is one suggestion from this chapter you can adopt in order to "party smart"?

CRAFTING YOUR RULE

1. Finish this sentence: A God-blessed party looks like . . .

2. What will you serve at this party you've described?

3. What will you do at this party?

4. How often will you throw a party like this?

5. Who can you invite that would least expect an invitation?

6. What will make partying right hard to do? What challenges do you anticipate to God-blessed celebrations?

7. Who can be your ally in doing this well?

8. What are you most afraid of as you move forward?

9. What is your strategy for dealing with that fear in a healthy way? Who will you talk about it with? What will your life look like without that fear?

CHAPTER 11

SEX

If you ever have to bring a room of unruly people to order, I have a great way to get everyone's attention. Start quietly whispering, "Sex, sex, sex," over and over again. People will stop what they're doing and strain to hear whether you're going to continue your thought because, hey, you're talking about sex, and sex is something we pay attention to. Actually, to say that we "pay attention" to sex isn't entirely true. We adolescently obsess over sex, we exploit sex, we leverage sex, but we rarely actually pay attention to it.

What is sex? What makes something sexual? Is it only the physical mechanics of intercourse or is it something more than that? When does routine physical contact become sexual contact? What standard do you employ to determine when something is sexy? How about too sexy? These are nuanced questions, and attempting to answer them can sometimes expose our inability to speak about sex well. For something everybody seems to be interested in talking about, it is hard to find conversations worth having. Has this been your experience?

Statistically, nearly half of all emerging adults graduating from high school will have already had sexual intercourse.[1] By the time they leave college or reach their mid-twenties, the numbers for those claiming to have had intercourse before marriage jump to 89 percent for men and 92 percent for women.[2] What these statistics indicate is that there is a strong social current in early emerging adulthood, and it moves toward having intercourse. The story seems to say, "Of course you'll have sex after high school," and if you don't "something must be wrong with you."[3]

But is it?

As early as the second century AD, one of the things distinguishing Christians from everyone else in their culture was their sexual self-discipline. The great Greek physician Galen noted in his writings from the time that Christians were known for the fact that they believed in the resurrection of the body, and that they didn't sleep around.[4] This practice of sexual restraint mystified onlookers like Galen because they didn't think life could be lived that way. It wasn't normal.

For those early Christians, something called chastity was actually part of their good news proclamation. I define chastity here in positive terms. Being chaste is about more than simply restraining from intercourse. Chastity is the spiritual discipline of bending your body into the flow of the gospel. For Christians, I believe this means intercourse and fidelity inside marriage and abstinence outside of it. But, chastity is also much more than this. Lauren Winner has written that chastity is "doing sex in the body of Christ. Doing sex in a way that befits the body of Christ and that keeps you grounded and bonded in the community."[5] Living chaste lives is one of the many ways over the years that Christians have announced that Jesus is King and God is actually running the show.

So, what do we do with the tension chastity creates in a culture that says if you're not having sex, something is wrong with you? The answer for some has been to dismiss sexual self-control as impractical and unrealistic. They try to relieve the tension by encouraging folks to sleep with whomever they choose as long as they use protection. But this makes Christians no different from anyone else. Others have taken a more heavy-handed approach, trying to resolve the tension through elaborate rules and boundaries about when, where, and how sexual expression can happen. But this can end up making sex feel like it's wrong, or even that your body is something to be ashamed of. Neither of these options is good enough for God's people. What if, instead, Christians today are called to *not* resolve the tension? What if the way to make the best choices about sex is from within the struggle and not by settling it? This would mean we need some tools for living chastely and building a helpful and healthy sexual ethic. That is precisely what I hope to provide in this chapter.

It is important to say up front that Don and I are starting with the view that sexual intercourse is still something that goes exclusively with marriage. We are running with a classical Christian position on this, and I don't plan to remake a case for it here in this chapter. First, because there's not enough space, and second because there are already excellent books on the topic (I have referenced a few in the endnotes). Instead I'd like to offer two additional tools that are designed to help communities pay better attention to sex and have conversations about it that are worth having.

Our Take...
Have Sex in Four Dimensions

A few years ago, I went to the French Quarter in New Orleans for the first time. If you've never been, it is a fascinating place. The neighborhood is made up of equal parts dance clubs, voodoo shops, restaurants, ghost tours, tourist traps, and street vendors, and the streets are filled with locals and visitors alike.

Upon entering the Quarter on my first day, my van passed a massive neon sign on top of a store that read "Relax, it's just sex." The store is run by Hustler (a pornography publisher), and the subtext of their announcement is this: "Hey, don't get all wound up about sex because, really, it's not a big deal. Sex is just two people enjoying themselves. It is simply a physical exchange; there's nothing more to it than that." But is this really the case?[6] Is intercourse really just skin on skin, or is there more to it than that? Does it only provide pleasure, or is there something unavoidably bigger going on? To answer Hustler's claim, we have to go back to the very beginning.

Christian conversations about sex have to start with the fact that our bodies are part of God's good creation. When God created human beings in His image, He made them with bodies[7] and those bodies are good. They are not in competition with God or dangerous to us. Our bodies are part of God's right-side-up ordering of the world, and that includes things they were made to do—eat, drink, sleep, and yes, even have sex.

The problem shows up in Genesis 3. In the onset of the good creation, human relationships to God, themselves, each other, and the creation itself were all intact and right-side up. Things were as they were meant to be. However, when human rebellion brought sin and death into creation, it flipped God's good world upside down. Suddenly the healthy and whole relationships that humans enjoyed in the good creation were fractured. Their relationship with God was broken (when God showed Himself, they hid[8]). Their relationship with themselves and their own bodies was fractured (they were ashamed of their nakedness[9]). Their relationship with each other was broken (when God asked what happened, each blamed the other[10]), and finally their relationship with the creation itself was broken (they had to leave the garden[11]). Isn't it sad that we have never known it any other way? What God started as good and whole, we more often experience as broken and backward.

Even though we're made to be connected in rich and satisfying ways, we live in a time where things are not the way they are supposed to be.

Now, the word *sex* is partially derived from the Latin word *secare*, which is a verb meaning "to cut" or to "cut off." This begs an interesting question about what sex is. What if sex and our sexuality includes both the recognition that we are "cut off" from the way things are supposed to be, and all the choices we make, trying to put things back together? From this perspective, sex could be defined as our energies for connection. In this way, the concept of sex includes both the awareness that we are disconnected as well as all the ways we go about trying to reconnect.[12] According to the Genesis story, this would make sex a four-dimensional reality. It is about how we reconnect to God, neighbor, self, and creation. In this way, the church's approach to sex is always going to be far bigger than just "doing it."

This is why I think Christians always sound off-key when they treat sexual ethics like it only involves intercourse management. Sex is bigger than that, better than that, and more mysterious than that. It has not just one application but four dimensions. Yes, intercourse is part of it, but when Christians focus solely on where "the line" is or what makes something "sex" or what doesn't (does oral sex count, etc.) they are letting Hustler set the terms of the debate, and that's just not good enough. God made sex, and as such, God's healing action in the world should be our compass for how we "do it" right.[13] Christians should therefore look for sexual healing in four dimensions.[14]

Going Public and Going Private

My parents moved to Durango, Colorado, some years ago, and every year my family and I travel out to visit them. There is a park downtown where my kids love to play, so on one visit we brought a picnic lunch and spent the morning playing before we ate. When lunchtime rolled around, there was nobody else in the park so we claimed a picnic table, pulled out the cooler, and started serving sandwiches. It was then that I noticed that a teenage couple had entered the park, dropped to the ground, and started going at it not ten yards from where we were sitting. They were in full-blown, four-alarm make-out mode and didn't care that anybody else was around. Our presence had no bearing on their behavior. So all four adults sat eating lunch, trying to pretend that what was happening within earshot wasn't happening, and crossing our fingers in hopes that the kids wouldn't ask any questions. Some of you may be thinking, *Well, why didn't you say anything to the teens?* The answer to that question is actually the point of this whole story.

Every culture has notions about what is supposed to be public and what is supposed to be private. These categories are socially determined and often exist without anyone explicitly stating what they are (for example, think about the social rules of using a public restroom). In our culture, we consider the sexual choices a person makes to be private. They are nobody's business but the couple involved. As such, what was happening on the ground behind me, even though it was in full view of a table full of people, was considered too private for me to acknowledge. There just isn't any common agreement or language in our culture for me to even begin to talk about why it was weird. And think about what would have happened if I had said something. Can't you just picture the looks of indignation on their faces? And why would they have been offended? Because in speaking to them I would have transgressed one of our society's unstated social contracts: a person's sexual choices are supposed to be private.

What is ironic about this is that you don't have to look very far to realize that sex in our culture is anything but private. Every time I need to get my computer serviced I go to the Apple store at the mall near my workplace. To get there, I must walk by Victoria's Secret where, in the store windows, there are images of at least a half dozen women in their underwear, featured in posters aimed at selling the latest styles of lingerie. This is a very public display of sex and sexuality, and it is indicative of the innumerable ways our culture puts sex out there to sell everything from clothing to cars. So, as much as we consider personal choices about sex to be private, we also have this very public dimension to how those choices can be expressed.

So, which is it? Is sex a public or private thing in our culture? The answer to this question is "Yes." Within most cultures in human history, sex and sexual discussions have had both a public and private dimension, the boundaries of which are determined by those unwritten rules of conduct I mentioned before. In today's Western culture, we regard the choices someone makes about what they wear and who they share their body with as being the private side of our sexuality; while the outward expression of those choices, in everything from revealing clothing to the teens rolling around in a park together, make up the public side. The question this raises for me is, how are Christians supposed to make sense of all this and make good choices in the midst of it? This is where Lauren Winner comes to the rescue.

In her book *Real Sex*, Lauren Winner asked a very profound question of our social agreements regarding sex and what we consider public and private.[15] What if, she contended, we've got it all backward? What if, for Christians, the sexual expressions our culture allows to be public are actually meant to be the most private? And what if the things society contends are the most private in regard to sex are actually supposed to be the most public? What if in God's right-side-up world, the outward expressions of sex, like exposed body parts, erotic language, and physical expressions of love are not for everyone to see but just a few. Conversely, what if our personal choices about where, when, and why we choose to have intercourse, dress in public, and visibly display our affection, are meant to be determined not alone but in community? This would make everything we assume is supposed to be private about sex public and everything we think is meant to be public private.

This flip can radically change the way we make sexual decisions, but in re-humanizing ways. We are not made for interdependence. We are designed for community. So, when we take the choices about our sex lives (which are an expression of found community—remember two bodies becoming one flesh) and make them autonomously, we lose a piece of how God created us to be. For many of the emerging adults I work with, this is the biggest challenge. Our consumer culture grooms us toward secrecy, self-fulfillment, and autonomy in our sex lives. However, the worst sexual decisions I've made (and have seen others make) were made secretly, selfishly, and alone. What if our conventional wisdom isn't very wise when it comes to sex after all? What if the best sex is, somehow and some way, a more public sex? What if sexual choices should be discussed transparently, openly, and unashamedly in community in order to move toward redeemed relationships?

This is not as far out as you might think.

Throughout history, it was the community that conferred the privilege of intercourse onto a newly married couple after their marriage vows were taken. In fact, in some ancient Jewish traditions, the bride and groom go and consummate their marriage *before* rejoining their guests for the rest of the reception. How's that for shaking up public and private in 2012? Maybe sex was designed to be more communal than any of us give it credit for. And I don't mean communal here in a narrow or perverse context (i.e., orgies and the like). I mean communal in the sense that, as with those Jewish weddings, the choices we make about when, how, and with whom we share our bodies are best made with others and not alone.

Now I want to recognize that some of you reading this may come from a place where your body was controlled or oppressed by religious language about sex and calls for accountability. That grieves me and I don't want to be misheard here. I'm not suggesting we create new rules to control one another. I am simply asking each of us to think about with whom we might start to talk about our sexual choices so that they can be made, in this way, more "publically." How might we engage our communities of faith, teachers, parents, and mentors to make our sexual decisions more public? What are the ways that can be done well? What are the ways that can be done poorly? By engaging the topic in this way, it might free us to make better, more whole sexual decisions and make for the best sex any of us have ever had.

Other-Centered Sex

I was interviewing a college student who told me her experience of sexual temptation in college was different than she expected. What she expected was the lure of sex to be about fulfilling personal pleasure, but that's not what tempts her most to have sex. Instead she described to me a barter system that exists between men and women on her campus. Women, she said, feel like they have to commit to certain kinds and/or amounts of sex acts in order to retain a commitment from men. If you want relationship, say these men, then "put out." Sadly, this woman I interviewed told me that she struggles with not giving into that pressure because, "I don't want to be alone."

Hearing her story made me angry. It is not right. It leaves this wonderful young woman feeling like she has to do something she doesn't want to because that's the way the system is set up. Furthermore, this social dynamic becomes a player in the shockingly high incidence of sexual assault that exists on college campuses.[16] Such sex degrades and dehumanizes both parties involved. It violates the healing and wholeness God desires for all four dimensions of human sexuality and, as a result, makes God grieve as well.

Because of this, I want to close this chapter with a challenge. Not to make a pledge or take a vow but simply to consider how you will love your neighbor as yourself with your sexuality. Could we at least begin by asking how each of us can use our God-given energy for connection to bring health and peace and wholeness to all the relationships in our lives? Might we consider the needs of another before our own by asking, "What will my sexual choices here teach this person about what it means to be a man or a woman?"

These are the questions of Christian chastity in our day, and they are meant to be asked and answered in community by single and married alike. This is because all of us have a responsibility to be sexual in ways that promote peace and beauty and even justice.[17] We can do it,[18] but we'll need each other along the way. Who can join you in making sexual decisions that glorify God?

THE WAY IN . . .

Watch Don's DVD clip on sex.

1. Who taught you about sex? How did they teach it?

2. How is sex usually talked about among your groups of friends?

3. Don suggests that sex is powerful because it creates bonds between people that really matter. Do you think this is true? Can you think of any examples of how sexual bonding could be misused? What about examples of how it could be used well?

4. From what you observe, how much do people consider the needs, health, and wholeness of another person when it comes to sex?

EXPLORING FURTHER . . .

1. What, if any, questions did this chapter evoke in you?

2. The author suggests that sex is more than just intercourse. Do you think this is true? Why or why not?

3. C. S. Lewis once said that chastity is the most unpopular of the Christian virtues.[19] Do you think he's right? Explain.

4. The author makes the case that the things in our culture considered private about sex should actually be public and the things we regard as public instead kept private. Does that resonate with you? Why or why not?

5. Does the author's call to make our sexual choices more public sound like good news or bad news to you? Why?

EXPLORING BLUE LIKE JAZZ

CRAFTING YOUR RULE

1. Consider your sexual history. If it would be helpful and healing, jot down any milestones that you feel have affected you the most. (If at any point in your life you have been sexually assaulted or touched sexually in a manner that was inappropriate or unwanted, please talk with your parents, your pastor, or a trusted adult right away.)

2. How do you make your sexual decisions? Why do you make them this way?

3. How do you make your choices about sex now? Who can you include or continue to include in the process to make sure your sex stays public in the right ways?

4. What do you think will be the hardest part about this? Who can help you?

5. Who will you talk to when the going gets tough?

CHAPTER 12

GO IN PEACE

My Roman Catholic friends refer to their Holy
Communion service using the shorthand title "Mass." The title is
a derivative of the Latin phrase that makes up the last sentence of
the liturgy, *Ite Missa est* or "Go! It is sent." What's cool about this
to me is that the Mass is designated for its dismissal. This means
that the whole worship service, from the singing to the sacrament,
is named for what happens not during the service but instead at the
end. The nourishment of the Eucharist is not the end in itself. It is
always looking toward the time when the people are dismissed to
be God's hands and feet in the world.

This seems like an appropriate way to conclude this book as
well—with a dismissal. This book is about how to live life well in
emerging adulthood. We have touched on many topics and given
not just food for thought, but space for personal reflection and
communal conversation—but now what? What's next?

You have two choices: One is to only remember the things
you have learned in this book and keep it as a reference for future
questions and teaching. That's a fine thing, but there is another
path. The second choice is to accept the challenge of this book to

build a meaningful and healthy life in emerging adulthood and then take some concrete steps toward doing so.

Living in the Desert

In the first chapter, I likened emerging adulthood to a desert with no roads or paths pointing the way across it. Living in such a desert can be dangerous, but it doesn't have to be. It all depends on how you approach it. Early on, many Christians chose to live in the desert and practice their faith with a tool called the *rule of life*.

A rule of life is a devotional arrangement wherein the Christian disciple makes intentional promises that govern and form the choices of his or her life. These areas have historically included group worship times, personal prayer, service to the poor, evangelism, hospitality, and alms giving. Their rule forms an intentional frame and structure for how faith is acted out. It accepts that maturity and healthy life choices do not happen by accident. Instead, they require purposeful and strategic selections so that the yes's and no's of our lives will move in sync with God's kingdom. The most famous Christian rules of life, like the Rule of St. Benedict, are made up of chapters that detail their content. To that end, Don and I have written five modern-day precepts that together form a great Rule of Life for Emerging Adults. These precepts together provide a frame and structure for living the Christian life well in the desert of post-adolescence; however, that's all they do—provide a frame. You fill in the details and specifics because, after all, it's your life we're talking about here.

Precept #1: Know Your Story

A few years ago, my dad needed to find a new doctor and on his first visit, he was asked to lay out our whole family's medical history. Any diseases his father, mother, uncles, aunts, cousins, and siblings had ever been diagnosed with had to be disclosed so the physician could make accurate diagnoses and make wise choices regarding his future treatment. As my father rattled off the names of his relatives who had struggled with cancer (of which there were many), the doctor put his clipboard down and asked straight-faced, "Did you grow up over a toxic waste dump or something?" Seriously, that's what he said! My dad roared with laughter and the two have been tight ever since. My point is this: in life, as in medicine, it is more important to know where you've come from than where you are going. If you're going to figure out anything about the future, you have to pay attention to the past. That's why the first precept in our rule of life involves knowing your story.

Your story is comprised of the big narratives you use to make sense of your life. This includes any inklings you have about "the meaning of life," as well as all the under-the-radar expectations that we use to define words like "normal," "success," "safety," and "failure."

For some, the hardest thing to believe is that our stories are not something we choose. We are actually born into them. They come from our families of origin and our socio-economic upbringing. They develop as we collect experiences as children and adolescents, and they continue to shape our lives as we age. The key to a balanced and intentional life in emerging adulthood must begin with a sober evaluation of where you have come from because that, like my dad's medical history, will determine where you are going.

All of Don's choices in *Blue Like Jazz* are driven by the story he inherited from his family of origin. His narrative is shaped by his parents' divorce, his father's liberal bohemianism, his conservative religious upbringing, and his mother's betrayal. It is not until he becomes aware of himself and where he is in his life story that he is able to find healing, purpose, and that all-important concept for this movie—freedom. When Don becomes conscious of how shaped he is by where he's come from, things start to change. The same is true for all of us too. This fine art of paying attention will free you to make choices that are intentional from the inside out. It's why knowing your story is so important.

Thinking It Through

The place to begin learning your story is by investigating your family of origin.

* Ask and answer questions like: Where did you come from? If you could describe the family you grew up with in three words, what would they be? What is the history of your family in your city? What kind of relationship did your parents have with their parents? Was communication valued in your family?

* Call your oldest living relative and ask him or her to tell you the oldest story they can remember.

* Why did you go to college? Or why didn't you go to college?

* Define the words *success* and *failure*. What will make you a success in your eyes? What will make you a failure? Where do your definitions come from? How much do your definitions connect to a job you have or want? Why is that?

Precept #2: Pick Your People

I had a friend in college whose accent would change depending on who she was spending time with. When she was with our friends from England for a weekend, her speech would take on a slight British affect. When she spent time with her family in South Carolina, a southern drawl would emerge in her speech patterns. One day we asked her if she realized that she was doing it, and she said, "No! But I suppose you're right—I do change accents, don't I? I hadn't realized that until you pointed it out to me."

But this isn't so surprising, is it? The people we hang out with influence us, whether we know it or not. Sometimes this influence is for the better (think twelve-step recovery or domestic abuse support groups) and sometimes for worse (add your own examples here.) You've heard it said, "You are what you eat," but I say, "You are who you hang out with."[1]

Watching Don in *Blue Like Jazz* is like a case study for this maxim. When he arrives at Reed, he is an open book. Yes, he is angry and reactive, but he is receptive to new ideas and experiences. So everything he tries on for size, from the pope's cynicism to Penny's activism, is influenced by his new friends. Don doesn't read about new lifestyles and then, after academically weighing their benefits and drawbacks, render a judgment. No! He sees people living a certain way and, because he trusts them, he joins in. I think we can all relate to that.

None of our ideas, beliefs, or actions exist in a vacuum. The people in our community influence us and we influence them. Sometimes these effects are wonderful and sometimes they are toxic, which is why we must pick our friends carefully because they will help shape who we are. However, positive communities are just the beginning. It is also necessary to find a good mentor.

Remember those early desert Christians? They lived their rule of life under the direction of an abbot or abbess, and maybe this is good advice for us too. Find someone older and wiser in the faith than you to offer some direction and leadership on your journey. When picking a mentor, you want to look for someone who is going a similar direction. Think of them like a scout rather than a guide. Someone on the same trail you're on, but just a little farther down the path. A good mentor will not tell you what to do but will instead ask open-ended questions in order to help you reflect on your choices. He or she will expect vulnerability from you, and you should expect challenges from them, because the process of being mentored is active. It will require action and intent on your end, and rising to this challenge is part of what will form you. Like picking the right community, finding a mentor is hard work, but well worth the effort.

Thinking It Through

Finding the Best Mentor

* The way you'll locate the right person is first by being observant in your own life. Pay attention to the leaders of your different circles. You can find mentors in anyone from a professor, a pastor, or even an older friend. Make a list of potential mentors before you ask one.

* Remember that this person has a whole life outside their interaction with you, so approach them with humility and gratitude. If they meet with you, it is a gift they are giving. You are not entitled to it.

✳ Learning about the person you want to be your mentor will help you know how to ask them. How well you know them can help determine if a face-to-face meeting will be better than an email or phone call.

✳ Don't give up if the first person you ask says no.

✳ Expect to meet once a month initially. Being mentored requires patience, and part of its formation requires learning that things don't always come on your terms.

Finding the Best Community

✳ Connect with fellowship groups, churches, and families in your area to find a community to support you. When I was in college I couldn't find a fellowship group to connect with, but a family from the youth ministry I volunteered with became my anchoring community. Is there already someone in your life who can provide a tether?

✳ What community currently has the most influence in your life? How do you see that influence manifest? Do you think it is positive or negative? How can you tell the difference?

Precept #3: Practice Moderation

You may have heard it said, "All things in moderation, including moderation,"[2] and actually that is really good advice. One of the hardest things to have perspective on as an emerging adult is that everything you do actually matters. The patterns and habits you develop now will remain with you as you grow older. There is no magic finish line where our vices are left effortlessly behind.

In the movie, Don's relationship with alcohol swings from one extreme (his non-drinking Baptist roots) to another (binge drinking). This pattern mirrors what many EAs experience in college where the only options seem to be total abstinence or over-indulgence. Have you ever seen this happen? Whatever was white during high school becomes black in college, or whatever was black swings over to white. This pattern of extremes is not just limited to the usual suspects of alcohol and drugs either. It can also happen with technology (how many hours a day are you on Facebook?) new ideas and ideologies (do you have any friends who change their lives with every new book they read?), and relationships. This all-or-nothing approach is not maturity. It is the trading of extremes—and extremes are unsustainable.

This is why moderation is part of our rule. A healthy life will practice moderation but recognize that moderation takes training. Don't panic if you fail once or twice. Failure does not mean you are a disappointment and should head out on a bender. Instead, come back to your people, remember your rule, and talk to your mentor. Tell them what happened; make right any relationships you've broken and start again. Tomorrow is a new day and God's mercy is new every morning.

Thinking It Through

* What are your strengths and weaknesses?

* What do you do to relax?

* Is there any substance (alcohol, food, sleep aids, caffeine, other) you feel you have to use "just to make it"?

* What would a balanced and sustainable relationship with this substance look like (assuming this is a legal substance)?

* Who could you talk to about this to help establish boundaries in this area of your life?

* What are the things you are becoming extreme about?

* Are there things you will sacrifice exercise, sleep, healthy food, and a life free of debt in order to have over and over again?

* How do you define *moderation*? Does it have a positive or negative ring to it? Why do you think that is?

Precept #4: Find a Groove

I've been in bands ever since I was a teenager, and even though I've always played rock music, what I'm secretly enamored of is jazz. I fell in love with jazz because, quite frankly, I can't play it. The way the music fits together and the parts overlap yet complement each other is something I cannot reproduce. However, one thing I did get about jazz was the way the musicians played it by listening to each other. My years in rock bands had taught me how you have to listen to your bandmates in order to know when to play and when to hold back. Jazz players call this sitting "in the groove," and that groove is what anchors the music. Our lives need to "sit in a groove" as well. We need to be intentional about having balance in our activities and be wise about when we add things to our schedules and when we hold back. This balance between having too much and too little on our plates is what this precept in your greater rule of life is all about.

Emerging adulthood is frequently a time when one has the most control over their schedule and much free time to fill. So, the question is, what are you filling your time with? To further the music metaphor, what sets your life's tempo or speed? Do you have a standard that helps determine what is too fast or too slow? Do you know how to let that which does not matter truly slide?[3] What does your calendar look like?

Answering these questions can help us know when to "play our instrument" by adding something new to our schedules and when to "hold back" by saying no. They can also help us determine when we are doing too much and when we are doing too little. Work through the questions below and show them to a friend or mentor.

Crafting a healthy schedule takes intention, but it is well worth the effort. The habits and rhythms you learn now will last a lifetime.

Thinking It Through

✳ Get a sheet and paper and chart out every day of your week. Now start to fill in the spaces in the week with your commitments. What did you start with? Was it school or work related? Why do you think you began with what you did?

✳ Make a list of what you do in a week that makes you feel human. These are the activities that are life-giving to you. (This can be everything from taking trumpet lessons to listening to music with friends to a weekly Bible study).

✳ Make a list of what you *have* to do every week (school, work, taking out the trash, etc.).

✳ Now take that calendar of the week and start to fill in your hours. How can you include both your "have to's" and "need to's" in a way that allows your humanity to flourish?

✳ Have you included exercise and eating healthily?

✳ What part does joining your community for worship play in your week?

✳ Where are you serving others during your week?

✳ How does prayer factor into your day and week?

* What do you need to cut out of your week in order to make time for what matters?

* Show your schedule to a trusted friend or mentor. Ask them if they think you are "in the groove."

Precept #5: Be a Good Friend

I was asking the twentysomethings I work with about friendship and every one of them told me the same thing: true friendships are extremely important and really difficult to come by. Because many EAs live far away from the family and social networks they had in adolescence, their new friendships take on added weight and importance. Friends become like family. Yet as important as friendships are, what it takes to find and keep a good one is still a mystery to many. Even EAs who have a healthy community are sometimes at a loss for how it got that way in the first place. For this reason, the final precept of this rule of life involves some simple tools for cultivating and keeping healthy friendships.

First, be a friend and not a judge. Have you ever run across someone who was worried that hanging out with a friend without first condemning a certain behavior of theirs was the same as condoning it? Have you ever been that person? If so, take a deep breath. Nothing could be further from the truth. When friends and family are in the midst of making bad choices (or are hurting because of the consequences), they need an ally and not an adjudicator. They need someone to first demonstrate the mercy of God, not to tell them, "I told you so." By acting as a judge we ignore one of Jesus' most famous teachings to attend to the plank in our own eye before removing the speck of dust from our neighbors.[4] This is not to say there is not a time and place for hard conversations. Just remember—God's help always starts as grace, so ours should as well.

Second, fight well. For many, even a small fight in a relationship is a deal breaker because they lack even basic skills for working through conflict. This actually contributes to the sense of isolation many EAs experience because working through conflict is what builds intimacy. So use a few simple strategies like listening to gain understanding (instead of to determine right and wrong), avoiding the use of "always" and "never" (nobody "always" does anything), avoiding assumptions about someone else's motives (you cannot read minds no matter how sure you might be), and offering forgiveness (which is different than saying "It's okay"), making space for the reconciliation and healing that allows a relationship to go the distance.

Third, know the difference between a confidante and a counselor. When we live interdependent lives, things can get messy. It's important that we are present with one another in times of pain, however, that presence must have healthy boundaries. Because most of us are not trained counselors and we cannot "fix" our friends' pain, we should not attempt to do so. Be there with your friends in their times of darkness, but also know when to it's time to step back and find professional help.

Fourth, be a servant. Spend time promoting someone else's personal growth. This can be serving in a soup kitchen, volunteering in a youth ministry, or becoming a mentor. Just do something with your time that benefits someone else. Many EAs get a bad rap for being self-centered and narcissistic. Don't encourage that stereotype by fulfilling it. Be the kind of friend you want others to be to you and you'll be off to a great start.

Thinking It Through

* When you have conflict with someone else, what is your first inclination? Do you talk about it, ignore it, blow up, or get passive-aggressive? Where do your conflict management skills come from?

* Identify the professional resources available to you so that if there were a crisis, you would know where to go for help. Make some bookmarks on your Web browser with numbers for suicide hotlines and addiction recovery centers. Ask an adult you trust for the recommendation of some good counselors.

* Where are you acting as a role model? If you're not helping anyone else along in their journey, why not?

✴ Are you serving others anywhere in your life right now? If not, to whom can you talk about getting involved?

✴ Who do you think sees you as a role model? What do they see?

As you move through these precepts and craft your own rule of life, remember that God will never give up on you. No matter what you do or say. No matter the questions, doubts, or wonton rejections you throw at Him. No matter your successes or failures, God will never give up on you. No matter what, there will always be space to come home and start again.

Always.

No.

Matter.

What.

Now, go in peace to love and serve the Lord.

WISDOM
FOR THE ROAD

Remember when you were a kid and as you were
leaving your house someone called after you and said, "Hey, I have
one more thing to tell you before you go"? What they had to say
was usually superfluous and not anything you necessarily needed
to be told ("Be careful!" "Buckle your seat belt!" "Be good"), but
the fact that they shared meant they loved you so you tolerated it.
That's what this part is. It's the one thing I wanted to tell you before
you go. It may be stuff you already know and would do anyway
(like being careful, or wearing your seatbelt) and it may do no good
(you're going to make your own choices anyway), but just humor
your old friend here and know that I'm only calling after you out of
love. Now where was I? Oh yes . . .

I have one of those GPS apps on my smart phone and I use it
all the time. One of its coolest features is the way it syncs up with
local radar to show where the traffic is heavy and where it is light.
A red line down your road means things are backed up, while a
green line means it's going to be smooth sailing. This has helped me
pick the right way to get around town and kept me from getting
stuck unnecessarily. The following are a few pieces of wisdom that
should work like a GPS to keep your route through emerging

adulthood as "green" as possible. These are not gimmicks, but rather some traveling wisdom accumulated from folks who hit a lot of "red lines" in the twenties and would do it differently next time around.

Remain Teachable

No matter how much you agree or disagree with someone or his or her ideology, remember, everybody can teach you something. Everyone has wisdom to share. So, pay attention, be alert, and remain teachable. Not everything you learn during this phase of life will come from a class, nor will it all come from sources you have already determined to work for you. Many EAs shut down when they run across someone whose worldview does not already agree with their own. My advice? Don't shut down. Engage the new ideas and find the balance between passive consumption and out-of-hand dismissal. The former is born out of apathy, and the latter out of fear; neither of which will help you if you actually want to learn something. Remaining teachable keeps it green.

Everything You Do Matters and Nothing You Do Matters

There are two popular misconceptions about emerging adulthood. The first is that it is the most important and formative time of your life. The story goes that you have to get this part of your life exactly right or things will go cosmically off course. This is just not true. Yes, life in your twenties will be extremely formative, but no more so than any other phase of your life. The trick to all this is to pay attention to how you are being formed at every phase of your life (from emerging adulthood through retirement) and ask yourself, "Is this a good or bad thing?" So, while emerging adulthood is certainly a formative season, it is no more so than any other because nothing you do *really* matters.

However, this doesn't mean that emerging adulthood is a time of consequence-free independence. That is misconception number two. There are stories out there that will tell you, "Nothing you do (from sex to studying) really matters (meaning it won't have a consequence), so do whatever you feel like." This is also untrue. The moral and ethical choices you make now will form the habits that make up your character, which will shape the kind of person you become in the future. The patterns, values, and routines you develop now will stay with you for the rest of your life. Bad habits do not magically disappear when one gets married or reaches age thirty. In fact, they can become more concentrated and intense the older you get. In this sense everything you do matters, so just make sure to pay attention to what you're doing.

Fail Well

In 2010, comedian Conan O'Brien had a very public falling out with the network he had worked with for more than fifteen years. After they gave him his dream job (hosting *The Tonight Show*), they broke their contract and gave it back to the previous host due to Conan's sagging ratings. In the months that followed, it was fascinating to watch Conan work out his grief as honestly, hilariously, and publically as he did. In the spring of 2011, O'Brien was invited to give the commencement address at Dartmouth University, and what did he choose to talk about? Failure. Drawing on his own experience, Conan crafted a beautiful and hilarious reflection on the reality of disappointment, saying, "There are few things more liberating in this life than having your worst fear realized. . . . Disappointment will come. [But through it] you can gain clarity, and with clarity comes conviction and true originality."[1]

What all of us need to remember is that failure is inevitable. It is an inescapable part of the human experience, so we don't need to be afraid of it. No matter how well someone constructs a rule of life or how closely someone follows his or her life plan, mistakes will be made. Lapses in judgment and foolish choices are inevitable. You will not win every time. The question is, what will you do when you realize you've failed? Will you quit? Or will you accept the reality of your disappointment and work to bring something original, creative, and even beautiful out of it? Every one of us fails.

However, those of us who make it to the other side follow the lead of people like Conan O'Brien. We accept our failure for what it is, grieve the disappointment, and then look for how something good can be brought forth from it.

That's it.

You kids can go now.

Have fun.

Be safe.

Buckle your seat belt and live a life that makes things here on earth the way they are in heaven.

FIVE-WEEK BIBLE STUDY APPENDIX

Each session of this Bible study makes use of an ancient Christian tool for studying the Bible called *Lectio Divina*. While not following the *Lectio* format officially, each week does begin with a multi-voiced reading coupled with a time of silence and listening. Do not be afraid of this silence. Settle into it and let it go a little long if you can. Part of the benefit of this study is the time spent listening to what God's Spirit will speak to your heart. Give God the space to speak to you.

Session #1: Know Your Story

Song of David.

> [1]ALWAYS I will lift up my soul to You, Eternal One,
> [2]BECAUSE You are my God and I put my trust in You. Do not let me be humiliated. Do not let my enemies celebrate at my expense.
> [3]CERTAINLY none of the people who rely on You will be shamed, but those who are unfaithful, who intentionally deceive, they are the ones who will be disgraced.

⁴DEMONSTRATE Your ways, O Eternal One. Teach me to understand so I can follow.

⁵EASE me down the path of Your truth. FEED me Your word because You are the True God who has saved me. I wait all day long, hoping, trusting in You.

⁶GRACIOUS Eternal One, remember Your compassion; rekindle Your concern and love, which have always been part of Your actions toward those who are Yours.

⁷Do not HOLD against me the sins I committed when I was young; instead, deal with me according to Your mercy and love. Then Your goodness may be demonstrated in all the world, Eternal One.

⁸IMMENSELY good and honorable is the Eternal; that's why He teaches sinners the way.

⁹With JUSTICE, He directs the humble in all that is right, and He shows them His way.

¹⁰KIND and true are all the ways of the Eternal to the people who keep His covenant and His words.

¹¹O LORD, the Eternal, bring glory to Your name, and forgive my sins because they are beyond number.

¹²MAY anyone who fears the Eternal be shown the path he should choose.

¹³His soul will NOT only live in goodness, but his children will inherit the land.

¹⁴ONLY those who stand in awe of the Eternal will have intimacy with Him, and He will reveal His covenant to them.

[15]PERPETUALLY my focus takes me to the Eternal because He
will set me free from the traps laid for me.

[16]QUIETLY turn Your eyes to me and be compassionate
toward me because I am lonely and persecuted.

[17]RAPIDLY my heart beats as troubles build on the horizon.
Come relieve me from these threats.

[18]SEE my troubles and my misery, and forgive all my sins.

[19]TAKE notice of my enemies. See how there are so many
of them who hate me and would seek my violent
destruction.

[20]Watch over my soul, and let me face shame and defeat
UNASHAMED because You are my refuge.

[21]May honor and strong character keep me safe. VIGILANTLY
I wait for You, hoping, trusting.

[22]Save Israel from all its troubles, O True God.

Get two volunteers to read.

Begin by having the first volunteer read Psalm 25 aloud while
everyone listens.

Have the next reader read the psalm out loud again. This time,
ask the group to write down or remember a word or phrase that
stands out to them from the reading.

Have everyone share his or her word or phrase.

Now ask the group: What do you think the point of the psalm is?

Verses 4 and 5 say:

> Demonstrate Your Ways, O Eternal One
> Teach me to understand so I can follow.
> Ease me down the path of Your truth.
> Feed me Your word
> Because You are the True God who has saved me.
> I wait all day long, hoping, trusting in You.

What do you think the psalmist meant by "Teach me to understand" and "Ease me down the path of Your truth"?

When you hear words like God's "paths" and "truths," what do you think about first (rules, doctrines, etc.)? Now take turns reading the psalm one last time. Move clockwise around your group giving each person a chance reading a verse aloud in order until you have completed the psalm.

How many verses are there in the psalm?

Did you know that there are also twenty letters in the Hebrew alphabet? Each verse of this psalm begins with a letter of the Hebrew alphabet. One verse for each letter, in sequence. This is what's called an acrostic. By crafting the psalm this way, the author was saying something very intentional.

Look at the references in the psalm to God's "ways" and "paths." These are references to the Law given to the people of Israel. The

Law was considered a gift because it was a revelation about how to be truly human. God has shown the people how to live life right. But living well includes so much more than just following rules, doesn't it? This is why the psalmist used an acrostic to write this psalm. He was saying, in essence, that life works best when all its "A to Z-ness" is oriented around God's life and His story. God's story is about healing the world.

Watch Don's DVD clip called "Know Your Story."

1. Are "fate" and "destiny" real things, or do we have control over our lives?

2. How important is it to be intentional about how you live? What makes intentionality easy? What makes it difficult?

3. Don suggests that people who make a great story with their lives do so in three ways:

   • They know what they want.

   • They will make sacrifices to get what they want.

   • They will work through and overcome the conflicts that arise.

4. Do you agree with Don's assessment?

Consider Psalm 25 again:

5. How does Don's call to live life intentionally overlap with the psalmist's admonition to orient the whole "A to Z-ness" of your life around God's ways?

6. Have you ever seen someone who knew what they wanted, made sacrifices to get it, and endured the conflicts that came their way, but their story only helped them? Or worse yet, it hurt others? Share briefly.

7. How do you know the story you are living is going to be part of God's solution and not part of the world's problem?

Read Revelation 21:1–5.

8. This is a picture of God's future.

9. What are some of the ways you've seen others live their lives so that this picture of where things are going started happening in the present?

10. What are you living for? What direction is your story taking?

11. Is life happening to you, or are you living with intention?

12. How can your choices make this picture of God's healed world happen now?

Close with an extended period of silence. To end, go around the group and invite everyone to offer a one-word prayer in response to what God has shown them during this time.

Session #2: Pick Your People

Text: Ephesians 4:17–32

Therefore, as a witness of the Lord, I insist on this: That you no longer walk in the outsiders' ways—with minds devoted to worthless pursuits. They are blind to true understanding. They are strangers and aliens to the kind of life God has for them because they live in ignorance and immorality and because their hearts are cold, hard stones. And now, since they've lost all natural feelings, they have given themselves over to sensual, greedy, and reckless living. They stop at nothing to satisfy their impure appetites.

But this is not the path of the Liberating King, which you have learned. If you have heard Jesus and have been taught by Him according to the truth that is in Him, then you know to take off your former way of life, your crumpled old self—that dark blot of a soul corrupted by deceitful desire and lust—to take a fresh breath and to let God renew your attitude and spirit. Then you are ready to put on your new self, modeled after the very likeness of God: truthful, righteous, and holy.

So put away your lies and speak the truth to one another because we are all part of one another. When you are angry, don't let it carry you into sin. Don't let the sun set with anger in your heart or give the devil room to work. If you have been stealing, stop. Thieves must go to work like everyone else and work honestly with their hands so that they can share with anyone who has a need. Don't let even one rotten word seep out of your mouths. Instead, offer only fresh words that build others up when they need it most. That way your good words will communicate grace to those who hear them. It's time to stop bringing grief to God's Holy Spirit; you have been sealed with the Spirit, marked as His own for the day of liberation. Banish bitterness, rage and anger, shouting and slander, and any and all malicious thoughts—these are poison. Instead, be kind and compassionate. Graciously forgive one another just as God has forgiven you through the Liberating King.

Read Ephesians 4:17–32 aloud to the group and invite everyone just to listen.

Read it aloud once more.

Invite everyone in the group to share something from the text that stuck out to them.

Would it surprise you to learn that this letter to the Ephesians was written in the third-person plural? It was written to a community for a community.

The author of Ephesians expected people to grow and change as they related to one another in a community of faith. The way they were trying to live—the Jesus way—cannot be done alone. The phrase "take off your former way of life" is a call for transformation. But it is a call for transformation that takes place in community, because the kind of people we hang around with affect the kind of people we become.

Watch Don's DVD clip called "Pick Your People."

1. Can you find two places that Don's video and the Ephesians text overlap?

2. Don says that you will be like the people you hang around. Do you think this is true?

3. Can you think of an example when you have seen individuals influence one another in negative ways? What about positive ways?

Quoting the Greek poet Meander, Paul wrote in 1 Corinthians 15:33–34: "But don't be so naïve—there's another saying you know well—Bad company corrupts good habits. Come back to your senses, live justly, and stop sinning. It's true that some have no knowledge of God. I am saying this to shame you into better habits."

4. If bad company corrupts good habits, do you think the opposite is true as well?

5. Is it possible to be an influence on someone's life without coming off as arrogant or controlling?

6. Who has permission to speak into your life? How did they get that permission?

Close with an extended period of silence. To end, go around the group and invite everyone to offer a one-word prayer in response to what God has shown them during this time.

Session #3: Practice Moderation

Text: 1 Corinthians 10:6–25

Look at what happened to them as an example; it's right there in the Scriptures so that we won't make the same mistakes and hunger after evil as they did. So here's my advice: don't degrade yourselves by worshiping anything less than the living God as some of them did. Remember it is written, "The people sat down to eat and drink and then rose up in dance and play." We must be careful not to engage in sexual sins as some of them did. In one day, 23,000 died because of sin. None of us must test the limits of the Lord's patience. Some of the Israelites did, and serpents bit them and killed them. You need to stop your groaning and whining. Remember the story. Some of them complained, and the messenger of death came for them and destroyed them. All these things happened for a reason: to sound a warning. They were written down and passed down to us to teach us. They were meant especially for us because the beginning of the end is happening in our time. So let even the most confident believers remember their examples and be very careful not to fall as some of them did. Any temptation you face will be nothing new. But God is faithful, and He will not let you be tempted beyond what you can handle. But He always provides a way of escape so that you will be able to endure and keep moving forward. So then, my beloved friends, run from idolatry in any form. As wise as I know you are, understand clearly what I am saying and determine the right course of action. When we give thanks and share the cup of blessing, are we not sharing in the blood of the Anointed One? When we give thanks and break bread, are we not sharing in His body? Because there is one bread, we, though many, are also one body since we all share one bread. Look no further than Israel and the temple practices, and you'll see what I mean. Isn't it true that those who eat sacrificial foods are communing at the altar, sharing its benefits? So what does all this mean? I'm not suggesting that idol food itself has any special qualities or that an idol itself possesses any special powers, but I am saying that the outsiders' sacrifices are actually offered to demons, not to God. So if you feast upon this food, you are feasting with demons—I don't want you involved with demons! You can't hold the holy cup of the Lord in one hand and the cup of demons in the other. You can't share in the Lord's table while picking off the altar of demons. Are we trying to provoke the Lord Jesus? Do we think it's a good idea to stir up His jealousy? Do we have ridiculous delusions about matching or even surpassing His power?

There's a slogan often quoted on matters like this: "All things are permitted." Yes, but not all things are beneficial. "All things are permitted," they say. Yes, but not all things build up and strengthen others in the body. We should stop looking out for our own interests and instead focus on the people living and breathing around us. Feel free to eat any meat sold in the market without your conscience raising questions about scruples.

Get two volunteers to read.

Begin by having the first volunteer read Corinthians 10:6–25 aloud.

What are some of the questions you have after hearing this text? What do you think was going on in the community this was written to?

Have reader two read it one more time.

Paul was writing to address some very particular questions the Corinthian community had posed to him. One of them dealt with eating meat sacrificed to idols. Could they eat it or not? Paul's conclusion on the matter is found in verses 23–25. He said that although the idols were not real in the way God is real, and although he had told them earlier in the letter that they were free to eat of meat sacrificed to idols, in direct contradiction, he now said that they shouldn't eat the meat. What gives?

The reason for Paul's counsel here has to do with the spiritual care of new Christians in the Corinthian church. These young believers used to worship gods where the worship involved eating sacrificial meat. Therefore, if they saw a leader in their church eating that kind of meat, even though it's not spiritually dangerous, the young Christians might get the wrong idea. They may believe this church leader worshipped the idol instead of Jesus.

Now, reread verses 23–25. What did Paul tell them to do and why?

Paul wrote that even though they could eat this meat, they shouldn't in this case because it would hurt these young Christians. Although everything is permissible, not everything is beneficial. How can you tell when something you are doing is beneficial?

Watch Don's DVD clip called "Practice Moderation."

1. What overlap do you find between Don's call for moderation and Paul's teaching that just because you can do something doesn't mean you should?

2. What factors make practicing moderation hard?

3. Is there a way to take moderation too far?

4. Is there ever a place for over-indulgence in Christianity? If not, why? If so, when and where?

5. Where have you seen moderation practiced well? Where have you seen it practiced poorly? What's the difference?

Close with an extended period of silence. To end, go around the group and invite everyone to offer a one-word prayer in response to what God has shown them during this time.

Session #4: Find a Groove

Text: Ecclesiastes 10:18; Proverbs 10:4–5

The roof sags over the head of lazybones;
the house leaks because of idlehands. (Ecclesiastes 10:18)

A slack hand produces nothing by poverty,
but an industrious hand soon takes hold of riches.
A wise son stores up for the winter months while it is still summer,
But a shameful on lies around even during the harvest.
(Proverbs 10:4–5)

Ask three volunteers to read.

Have the first reader slowly read the two texts out loud two times. While the text is being read, invite everyone in the group to pay attention to the word or phrase that "shimmers" or "pops out" to them. Once they choose a phrase, have them begin to repeat it to themselves over and over.

Take a moment of silence. Then, go around the group inviting each person to share their word or phrase. Have the second reader read the text aloud again.

This time, ask everyone to consider what image or feeling is connected to the word or phrase they've been repeating.

Take another moment of silence. Then, invite each person in the group to share the image or feeling connected to their word or phrase.

Have your third reader read the text one last time.

Consider how the word or phrase and the image and feeling connects to your life right now. Offer an extended period of silence while people explore this in prayer. Invite individuals to share the connections they've made.

Watch Don's DVD clip called "Find a Groove."

1. What overlaps do you find between what Don says on the DVD and the biblical text for today?

2. Don says in the DVD that we need to take responsibility for our boredom. If you are bored as an adult, perhaps it's because you are a boring person. Do you think that is true?

3. When does staying in a good rhythm of life and not getting lazy turn into getting too busy? How can you tell the difference?

4. Slothfulness is a sin that the Roman Catholic theology identifies particularly with avoiding responsibility. Have you ever felt slothful? What did you do about it?

5. What's the place for Sabbath in a good rhythm of life?

6. As a group, brainstorm three or four healthy ways you can break out of boredom.

Close with an extended period of silence. To end, go around the group and invite everyone to offer a one-word prayer in response to what God has shown them during this time.

Session #5: Be a Good Friend

Text: Proverbs 12:26; Proverbs 17:17; Proverbs 18:24; Proverbs 19:6; Proverbs 22:24–25

Those who live right are good guides to those who follow,
but wrongdoers will steer their friends down the wrong path.
(Proverbs 12:26)

A true friend loves regardless of the situation, and a real brother exists to share the tough times. (Proverbs 17:17)

Someone with many so-called friends may end up friendless,
but a true friend is closer than a brother. (Proverbs 18:24)

Many try to win the favor of a generous person,
and everyone is a friend to someone who gives gifts. (Proverbs 19:6)

Do not befriend someone given to anger
or hang around with a hothead.
Odds are, you'll learn his ways, become angry as well,
and get caught in a trap. (Proverbs 22:24–25)

Go around the group and have everyone tell you who their closest friend is. What are three things about that person that makes him or her such a good friend?

Proverbs is a book of wisdom about how the world is and is meant to be. Above are five texts from it about friendship. Read them all aloud.

✳ Are all of the texts positive?

✳ Which descriptions of friendship above are most valuable to you?

✳ Which ones are the most difficult for you to embrace in order to be a good friend to others?

Watch Don's DVD clip called "Be a Good Friend."

1. Don suggests that the best way to make great friends is to be the kind of friend you want to have. Do you agree? Are friendships random, or can they be as strategic as he suggests?

2. Don offers three qualities that will make you a great friend:

- Don't gossip.

- Be there when they need you.

- Do what you say you're going to do.

3. What others qualities would you add?

4. Where do you see overlap between the Proverbs description of good and bad friends and Don's description in the video?

5. What qualities do you value most in a friend?

6. What is one concrete thing you can do to be a better friend this week?

Close with an extended period of silence. To end, go around the group and invite everyone to offer a one-word prayer in response to what God has shown them during this time.

NOTES

Introduction: Growing Up
Is Getting Harder and Harder to Do

1. From the Latin:"to grow up."

2. Adolescence is popularly defined as the time of life beginning at age thirteen and ending at age nineteen.

3. These four markers are taken from Christian Smith and Patricia Snell's excellent book *Souls in Transition: The Religious and Spiritual Lives of Emerging Adults* (New York: Oxford Press, 2009). If this part of the Introduction excites you, then grab their book. You'll love it.

4. "Emerging adult" is the term we will be using to describe this new and unprecedented phase of life among eighteen- to thirty-year-olds. The term "post adolescent" first began appearing in literature (See K. Keniston, *The Young Radical: Notes on Committed Youth* [New York: Harcourt, Brace & World, 1968]). However, more recently researcher/author Jeffery Arnett has settled on the descriptor "emerging adult" for all those ages eighteen to thirty. Christian Smith and Patricia Snell were compelled to use Arnett's terminology in *Souls in Transition* (mentioned above) and their argument convinced us to take it up as well.

5. This is based on the 2005–2009 U.S. Census projections. The actual number at the time of this book's publication is probably closer to fifty million. http://factfinder.census.gov/servlet/STTable?_bm=y&-geo_id=01000US&-qr_name=ACS_2009_5YR_G00_S0101&-ds_name=ACS_2009_5YR_G00_&-_lang=en&-redoLog=false&-CONTEXT=st.

6. In my experience, people are asking questions about these things no matter what phase of life they are in.

Chapter 1: Alcohol

1. If you're getting nervous that a chapter on alcohol is the way we begin the topical portion of this book, hang on. Alcohol is only first on the list because I'm ordering these chapters alphabetically, but it's actually the least complete on its own. What I mean is, the tools for God-blessed drinking are actually found in several places throughout this book. I've already made an appeal for moderation as a life practice (in chapter 12). That's stop number one. However, talk about alcohol should also include conversations about how to celebrate well, so check out chapter 10 on partying. Also, look at chapter 6 on drugs where we invite some self-reflection as to why you want to use any drug in the first place. What this leaves us with are the very practical considerations of how to make a strategy for drinking alcohol that makes sense and embodies healthy moderation. See, not so bad?

2. Our intent here is not to make this case or argue about whether the wine Jesus drank had alcohol in it or not. If this is an issue for you, you can skip this chapter, but I advise reading it anyway. I think you might appreciate what we're saying.

3. Proverbs 23:19–21; Romans 13:12–14; I Corinthians 5:10–11; Galatians 5:19–21; Ephesians 5:18; I Timothy 3:1–3; Titus 1:6–8; I Peter 4: 2–3—These are just the overt references. There are lots of inadvertent references to drunkenness not being a good idea as well. Stories of the people of God and their enemies making bad choices while getting drunk or the spots in Proverbs and Psalms where drunkenness is used as a metaphor for unwise and foolishness behavior. Bottom line, drinking is fine—drunkenness not so much.

4. Ginna Clark "Nonconsensual Sexual Experiences and Alcohol Consumption Among Women Entering College," *J Interpersonal Violence*, February 2011, 26: 399–413, first published on March 17, 2010.

5. Ralph W. Hingson, Wenxing Zha, and Elissa R. Weitzman, "Magnitude of and Trends in Alcohol-Related Mortality and Morbidity Among U.S. College Students Ages 18–24, 1998–2005," *J Stud Alcohol Drugs Suppl.* 2009 July; (Supplement no. 16): 12–20. "Among college students ages 18–24, alcohol-related unintentional injury deaths increased 3% per 100,000 from 1,440 in 1998 to 1,825 in 2005."

6. http://www.collegedrinkingprevention.gov/media/NIAAA_Back_to_School_Fact_sheet_8_19_10.pdf.

7. When I say do not drink alcohol, I'm talking about the social consumption of alcohol. Having alcohol as part of a religious service etc. is a different matter altogether.

8. See section in chapter 6 titled "Breakin' the Law! Breakin' the Law!"

9. If this really gets your goat, find a friend or mentor and explore why you feel entitled to drink before you are of age, or why you feel you need to. What you discover may be more helpful and healing to you than any beer ever could be.

10. From the National Institute for Alcohol Abuse and Alcoholism (NIAAA) website: http://www.niaaa.nih.gov/FAQs/General-English/default.htm#safe_level.

> For most adults, moderate alcohol use—up to two drinks per day for men and one drink per day for women and older people—causes few if any problems. (One drink equals one 12-ounce bottle of beer or wine cooler, one 5-ounce glass of wine, or 1.5 ounces of 80-proof distilled spirits.)
>
> Certain people should not drink at all, however:
>
> - Women who are pregnant or trying to become pregnant
> - People who plan to drive or engage in other activities that require alertness and skill (such as driving a car)
> - People taking certain over-the-counter or prescription medications
> - People with medical conditions that can be made worse by drinking
> - Recovering alcoholics
> - People younger than age 21.

11. See http://pubs.niaaa.nih.gov/publications/FamilyHistory/famhist.htm for more information about the relationship between alcoholism and genetics.

12. Genesis 1–2.

13. Genesis 3:8.

14. Genesis 3:10–11.

15. Genesis 3:11–13.

16. Genesis 3:23–24.

17. Theologian Scot McKnight explores what the gospel looks like in all four of these relationships in his book *Embracing Grace: A Gospel for All of Us* (Brewster: Paraclete Press, 2005).

18. The problem I find with a "rules based" mentality about drinking is the same I find in a "rules based" mentality about sex. The whole enterprise becomes a game of how close can I get to the line (wherever it is) without going over. Which, of course, leads almost everyone who has ever tried this right over the line eventually (because there is a thrill in breaking the rules) and then into shame (because you end up hating yourself for not being stronger).

    Approaching choices like this in a relational manner makes space for everyone's specific context and struggles (I may be able to have two drinks and you none) while still calling for a consistent Christian ethic.

19. Exodus 6:6–7.

20. Matthew 26:29.

21. 1 Corinthians 11:25.

22. There are some neat resources for parents and teens (like http://www .thecoolspot.gov/) out there including one that helps you show your child how advertising affects our perception of alcohol. The one I'm referencing above is called the "Magic Potion Myth" from the NIAAA website: http://pubs.niaaa.nih .gov/publications/makeadiff_html/makediff.htm.

    "The 'Magic Potion' Myth. The media's glamorous portrayal of alcohol encourages many teens to believe that drinking will make them 'cool,' popular, attractive, and happy. Research shows that teens who expect such positive effects are more likely to drink at early ages. However, you can help to combat these dangerous myths by watching TV shows and movies with your child and discussing how alcohol is portrayed in them. For example, television advertisements for beer often show young people having an uproariously good time, as though drinking always puts people in a terrific mood. Watching such a commercial with your child can be an opportunity to discuss the many ways that alcohol can affect people—in some cases bringing on feelings of sadness or anger rather than carefree high spirits."

Chapter 2: Confession

1. If you're looking for a place to start corporate confession, the Episcopal Church's Book of Common Prayer has a great one. Pray it together with the groups you are a part of. Then at the end have the leader offer the absolution. That person acts as the "hearer" and does a great service to the group.

Let us confess our sins against God and our neighbor.

Silence may be kept.

Officiant and People together, all kneeling

> Most merciful God,
> we confess that we have sinned against you
> in thought, word, and deed,
> by what we have done,
> and by what we have left undone.
> We have not loved you with our whole heart;
> we have not loved our neighbors as ourselves.
> We are truly sorry and we humbly repent.
> For the sake of your Son Jesus Christ,
> have mercy on us and forgive us;
> that we may delight in your will,
> and walk in your ways,
> to the glory of your Name. Amen.
> *The Priest alone stands and says*
> Almighty God have mercy on you, forgive you all your sins
> through our Lord Jesus Christ, strengthen you in all
> goodness, and by the power of the Holy Spirit keep you in
> eternal life. Amen.

A deacon or lay person using the preceding form remains kneeling, and substitutes "us" for "you" and "our" for "your."

2. In the Hebrew Bible, Rosh Hashanah and Yom Kippur (Feast of Trumpets and the Day of Atonement—Leviticus 23:23–32) are communal activities of repentance. The people take part in these festivals as individual members by examining their own lives, but they always understand themselves to be members of a whole people. This is why atonement is made for the people as a whole, not simply for each individual. In 1 Kings 8:35 and 2 Chronicles 6:24–27, God accused the people as a whole of sinning against Him and God called *them* to repent. Furthermore, when God sent the Israelites into exile, it was because of "their" sin as a people. Not an aggregate of all their individual wrongs, but a judgment on the moral failure of the nation as a whole. The New Testament continues this in many of the Epistles. They were written to groups of people for their common life. Certain letters, like 1 and 2 Corinthians for example, call for both individual and corporate change of life.

Chapter 3: Consumerism

1. *Oxford Advanced Learners Dictionary*, 2011.

2. Following the Industrial Revolution, there was a proliferation of goods and services being made at lower prices that, coupled with an increased amount of leisure time for the working class, meant there was more stuff available, more people to buy it, and more time to use it.

3. Compare with the more than two thousand images people saw thirty years ago. Children make up most of the new emerging market. http://www.nytimes .com/2007/01/15/business/media/15everywhere.html.

4. And you probably paid extra money for that logo you put on your body. How is that?!

5. I've found this account in lots of places, but it has been documented most popularly in Steven D. Levitt and Stephen J. Dubner, *Freakonomics: A Rogue Economist Explores the Hidden Side of Everything* (New York: HarperCollins, 2009), 87.

6. For more on how "cool" is bought and sold, see the 2001 Frontline documentary *Merchants of Cool*, Thomas Frank's *The Conquest of Cool*, and *Branded: The Buying and Selling of Teenagers* by Alissa Quart.

7. Thanks to my friend Micah Weedman for this turn of phrase.

8. What is ironic is that companies hire people called "cool hunters" to identify these trends and help them change their products to match the trends they find in the underground. In my case, it wasn't long before retail giants began making clothing and shoes that "looked vintage" so students like me would buy their version, which was easier to find and always in my size. Where do you see this happen today?

9. Churches do this too, don't they? In their desire to be relevant, they can often become worshipers of cool as well.

10. Luke 12:13–21, 23.

11. Exodus 20:17.

12. For more on that, see organizations like Not For Sale (www.notforsalestore .org) and Behind the Label (www.behindthelabel.org).

13. For more on repenting of our irony, see Jedediah Purdy's *For Common Things*. For further reading on consumerism and its influence, see: Naomi Klein, *No Logo: No Space, No Choice, No Jobs* (New York: Picador, 2009); Thomas Frank, *The Conquest of Cool: Business Culture, Counterculture, and the Rise of Hip Consumerism* (Chicago: University of Chicago Press, 2008); Tyler Stevenson, *Brand Jesus: Christianity in a Consumerist Age* (New York: Seabury Books, 2007); Alissa Quart, *Branded: The Buying and Selling of Teenagers* (New York: Basic Books, 2004); The Story of Stuff—check out the video, downloads, and curriculum available for free at http://www.storyofstuff.com/.

Chapter 4: Culture

1. The premise of this chapter is seriously indebted to Andy Crouch's *Culture Making: Recovering Our Creative Calling* (Downer's Grove, IL: IVP, 2008). If you want to read more about how Christianity and culture go together, this book is for you!

2. Genesis 1:26–28.

3. More about this and how our right "ruling" and "subduing" of creation is what true worship is all about in N. T. Wright's *After You Believe*.

4. We've all seen bigger and more dangerous examples of what happens when the culture makes people go bad. What do you think the church's responsibility is regarding these realities? How can we use our creative power for good?

5. H. Richard Niebuhr, *Christ and Culture* (New York: Harper & Row, 1956). I am crudely recounting the types here and I fully admit I'm not dealing with either their subtleties or their nuance. Fans and scholars of Neibuhr, I ask for your patience.

6. You may have heard of Qumran because it's where something called the Dead Sea Scrolls were found. These scrolls contain some of the oldest copies of the Hebrew Bible and the beliefs and practices of the Essene community themselves. Why this matters is that much of the way the Essenes did life with God sounds an awful lot like how the earliest Christians did life with God. It's thought that the fledgling church found much in common with how the Essenes saw and did things.

7. Among the notable Desert Fathers and Mothers are Amma Syncletica of Alexandria, John Cassian, and John Crysostom.

8. Dan Brown owes the Gnostics a thank-you letter because without their writings there is no *DaVinci Code*.

9. My people, the mainline Protestant church, struggle with this in regard to issues of social equality and justice. Cutting-edge evangelical churches often struggle with this regarding consumerism and technology.

10. Ironically, much of our public conversation regarding religion in the United States feels like it's coming from people who are trying to bring this back. They either want Christian doctrines enforced by the state or want to prevent another religion from gaining the ability to enforce its doctrines through the state.

11. A great book that expands Niehbuhr's typologies for a post-modern world is Craig Carter's *Rethinking Christ and Culture: A Post-Christendom Perspective* (Grand Rapids: Brazos, 2007).

12. It can also be idolatrous. Because God is the redeemer, Christians trying to make that their job can sometimes kick God right out of the way expecting they can do the job better. It's the same reason we are commanded in the Scriptures not to judge. Judgment is God's job, not ours, and when we try to do

it we are ultimately being idolatrous. Is this why some Christian attempts to engage in "culture wars" have such bent and distorted results? We're taking the wrong approach.

13. If you have never heard Rage Against the Machine, go to YouTube and watch "Bulls on Parade" or "Testify." Both are excellent examples of Morello's playing, even if you don't care for the politics of it all.

14. It's called Magdalene and Thistle Farms and both are a prime example of what redeemed Christian culture making looks like. Check them out as well as the bath and body products that fund their residential programs here: http://www.thistlefarms.org/.

15. I've heard Doug Pagitt say this for years. It's a good line.

Chapter 5: Doubt

1. The philosophy word for the study of how we know things is *epistemology*.

2. I know this game has other, more acerbic names. But come on, I was ten years old when I learned it. This is the PG version.

3. Søren Kierkegaard's *Journals and Papers*, trans. Hong and Malantschuk (Bloomington, IN: Indiana University Press, 1999), 399.

4. For a much deeper and richer explanation on the connection between doubt and faith, see twentieth-century theologian Paul Tillich's *Dynamics of Faith* (New York: Harper & Row, 1957).

5. Lesslie Newbigin. *A Proper Confidence*.

6. John 6:67–68.

7. Mark 9:14–29, emphasis added.

8. A great resource for leading emerging adults through this kind of process is Sharon Parks's *Big Questions, Worthy Dreams: Mentoring Young Adults in Their Search for Meaning, Purpose, and Faith* (San Francisco: Jossey-Bass, 2000).

9. If you want another more current and post-modern exploration of the place of doubt in faith, read Pete's first book *How (Not) to Speak of God*. He does some

dense yet excellent work, upending conventional wisdom regarding doubt and faith. Once you're done with that, check out everything else he's done. He's a gift.

10. Pg. 145.

Chapter 6: Drugs

1. Thomas Nordegren, *The A-Z Encyclopedia of Alcohol and Drug Abuse* (Parkland, FL: Brown Walker Press, 2002), 327.

2. National Survey of Drug Use and Health, The NSDUH Report: June 19, 2008.

3. It is addictive but kind of in the same way alcohol or tobacco is addictive. One in eleven users will become addicted to marijuana; it is not neutral in its effect on the human body. http://drugfactsweek.drugabuse.gov/files/teenbrochure_508 .pdf.

4. It should be noted that the parable's hearers would have seen the priest and the Levite in the story sympathetically. These two would be rendered unclean if they (or even their shadow, some taught) touched the body and would become outcasts. Should they help or not? This was one of the biggest theological debates of Jesus' day. Do you break Torah to save a life or keep Torah and let someone die? The Pharisees held the former position while the Sadducees held the later. The priest and the Levite would have been Sadducees.

5. If you look at the order of things the Samaritan does, they are actually the inverse of what the robbers do. The Samaritan systematically undoes what the robbers do.

6. http://www.npr.org/2011/05/01/135813656/war-turning-mexican-kids-into -targets-or-killers.

7. The products the cartels bring in include marijuana, as well as "harder" drugs like cocaine and heroin.

8. I'm thinking particularly of Jesus' subversive teachings in the Sermon on the Mount, Matthew 5:38–48. Check out Walter Wink's famous and wonderful exploration of these texts in *Engaging the Powers: Discernment and Resistance in a World of Domination* (Minneapolis: Fortress, 1992), 175ff; and here in this 1993 sermon/ interview, http://www.csec.org/csec/sermon/wink_3707.htm.

9. Beginning with Paul's missionary journeys (Acts 23:1–11 is a particularly exciting example), including the subversive language used in the letters that became the New Testament (see endnote #3 in chapter 7 for more on this), continuing with the severe Christian persecution of the Roman Empire, and following through church history all the way up to present day. Be it the current persecution of Christians in other lands or the recent civil rights movement in our own, there are so many examples of Christians demanding God's justice by actually violating unjust laws and bearing the consequences. Even when those consequences meant losing their lives. You see, for Christians, death is not the worst thing that can happen to a person.

10. Something I'm not covering here is whether or not marijuana should be legalized. It is beyond the scope of this chapter to comment upon. However, should it be legalized, our relational ethic of alcohol seems to be the best way to approach it. Practice moderation and evaluate what kind of health and healing is coming from your usage.

11. I think this is where medical marijuana lives too. If it's not prescribed for you, it's not legal for you to take it. Whether it's Adderall or medicinal marijuana. Again, this is not where we cash in that chip.

12. I recognize the way that drug policy and prison reform can come into the conversation here. This is an avenue worth exploring, but for the sake of this chapter, I'm speaking broadly about pot's illegality, not the nuances of three-strike drug policies and mandatory minimum sentences.

Chapter 7: Evangelism

1. This chapter will be far from a comprehensive exploration of this topic. There are several excellent books that ask these same questions and come to helpful, inspiring conclusions. I am indebted to these and recommend them if you want to take this conversation to a deeper and more nuanced place. Brad Kallenberg's *Live to Tell: Evangelism for a Postmodern Age* (Grand Rapids: Brazos, 2002); Brian McLaren's *More Ready Than You Realize* (Grand Rapids: Zondervan, 2002); George Hunter's *The Celtic Way of Evangelism: How Christianity Can Reach the West . . . Again* (Nashville: Abingdon, 2000); and Lesslie Newbigin's *The Gospel in a Pluralistic Society* (Grand Rapids: Eerdmans, 1989).

2. Romans 10:9; 1 Corinthians 12:3; Phillipians 2:11.

3. Yes, the caesar spoke of his role as *lord* and *savior* of all. The early church intentionally co-opted many of the Roman terms (even the word *church* is a Roman term) and re-appropriated them subversively to describe what they were doing. If this interests you, check out Brian Walsh and Sylvia Keesmaat's *Colossians Remixed: Subverting the Empire* (Downer's Grove, IL: IVP Academic, 2004) and Richard Horsley's *Jesus and Empire* (Minneapolis, MN: Fortress, 2002) and *Paul and Empire* (Minneapolis, MN: Fortress, 1997).

4. Matthew 19:28.

5. Isaiah 53:5.

6. Acts 3:21.

7. Revelation 21:1–15.

8. This matters as much for communities as it does for individuals.

9. John 1:14.

10. 1 Thessalonians 1:5.

11. I picked up this anecdote from David Chronic's dynamite position paper on evangelism over at the Word Made Flesh website, http://www.wordmadeflesh.org/the-cry/the-cry-vol-9-no-4/evangelism/. If you only have time to read one thing on evangelism, start with this article.

12. A college student told me one time, "Many people in the church are afraid that people won't ask. But the truth is they do—all the time. People ask. If you're living it people will ask." I think this is a good reminder.

13. See chapter 3.

Chapter 8: Gender

1. http://abcnews.go.com/Health/baby-storm-raised-genderless-gender-dangerous-experiment-child/story?id=13693760.

2. Genesis 2:18.

3. I am trying to leave room here for faithful Christians who read their Bibles and see different roles for men and women in regard to leadership. I am not trying to enter that conversation here (there's not enough space). However, wherever you come down on the issue of gender in leadership, all Christians should stand together against any subjugation of one gender by another. As Jesus says, "You know that among the nations of the world the great ones lord it over the little people and act like tyrants. But that is not the way it will be among you. Whoever would be great among you must serve and minister. Whoever wants to be great among you must be slave of all" (Mark 10:42–44). His kingdom is marked by service, not domination. Let's *engender* that.

4. This word means hatred of women.

Chapter 9: Money

1. The four markers are finish of education, new family formation, stable career, and financial independence: see chapter 1.

2. Matthew 6:24.

3. Deuteronomy 8:11–20.

4. Deuteronomy 8:18.

5. Scriptures like Psalm 24:1 and 1 Chronicles 29:14 come to mind.

6. This includes our very lives—but that's a conversation for another time.

7. I'm cribbing this term from N. T. Wright's theology. I like it.

8. See chapter 3 on consumerism.

9. I want to say that I don't believe credit cards are an inherently "bad thing." They can be helpful when used properly. The problem comes when companies stretch the rules to take advantage of EAs and their debt and consumers use them as a way to spend more than they can afford. However, the abuse of a thing doesn't make the thing itself dangerous.

10. The principle is the amount of money you initially borrowed. So if what you bought cost one hundred dollars but you could only pay sixty dollars at the end

of the month, the principle of the amount you owe the credit card company is forty dollars.

11. When you make a purchase, consider whether or not you have enough money in your hand to buy it before you do. Some people use a cash-only system as a tool to help them avoid the credit card debt merry-go-round. The problem isn't the credit card inherently; it is buying more than one can afford. So, if you're able to deal with the temptation of a credit card, then get one. They are extremely useful. Just make sure to budget things so you can pay off your statement at the end of every month.

12. http://marketplace.publicradio.org/display/web/2010/08/10/pm-student-loans -overtake-credit-card-debt/ and *http://www.newsytype.com/1957-student-loans/*.

13. Well maybe I am—that's a conversation for another time.

14. Mark 12:41–44. Jesus asks for giving that is sacrificial and based on what you have. What will this teaching mean for you?

15. To get a handle on how to live within a budget, my wife and I used a "cash only" system for our first year of marriage. We bought a sectioned recipe holder and labeled each of the tabs with one of our monthly expenses. Then we looked at our account balance sheets and credit card statements to figure out how much we were spending each month and on what. Then when our paychecks came in at the end of each month, we cashed them and filled each slot with the appropriate amount. On this system, I remember when the money was gone for the month, it was just gone! Unless we were going to make a sacrifice in one area, we could not splurge in another. This was just another tool for using your money to the glory of God.

16. Some examples are Matthew 6:1–4; Mark 12:41–43; and (don't take this one too far but . . .) Matthew 25:31–46 as well. Some examples in the early church are: Acts 4:32–47; 11:27–30; 2 Corinthians 9:1–15.

17. Leviticus 27:30; Number 18:21; Deuteronomy 12:6–7; 14:27–28.

18. Again, the story of the widow in Mark 12:41–43.

19. Again, Acts 4:32–47.

20. 2 Corinthians 8:1–5. In the Old Testament, the corollary to this is the feast of firstfruits in Leviticus 23:9–14. Here the first sheaf of grain you harvest is offered

in the temple *before* you eat it. Imagine this: you've not eaten fresh food all winter, but when the first of the harvest emerges in the spring, you just give it away. This is a profound act of trust because your food was your life. To hand over the firstfruits sends a message to the worshiper, and to God that says, "I trust You to bring the rest of what I need." This is to be our posture when we look at how to give things away. We don't have to be afraid that we won't have enough, because God will bring the rest of what we need. There is always enough.

21. Mathew 23:23–24.

22. For example, in order to sell a tomato when it is not being harvested in my region of the country, my supermarket has to buy tomatoes that have been grown in another part of the world. These tomatoes have to then be flown as many at two thousand miles and be chemically ripened so they can be sold year round. In my opinion, the problem in all this is not my grocery store—it's me. If I want fewer chemicals in my food, I have to consider that just because I can eat a tomato in the middle of January doesn't necessarily mean I should

23. Earlier this year I visited a museum display detailing life in Middle America during World War II. Because of rations there was a much different mind-set about how to use products than we have today. The motto was "Use it, wear it out or make it do." What a powerful corrective to our current "throwaway" culture. How many times have I bought a new pair of shoes before my old ones were used up? How many times have I truly worn out a pair of pants before buying a new pair? If you want a place to start using your money justly, why not adopt this slogan as your compass? My wife was so taken by this slogan that she hung it on our refrigerator. She said she sees the other messages about how to consume products enough that she wants to remind our family that there is another way to do things. Also, check out organizations like The One Campaign, International Justice Mission, and Bread for the World. These are Christian groups seeking to make God's economic justice a reality.

Chapter 10: Partying

1. For more on drinking well in emerging adulthood, see chapter 1.

2. All these stats are from a 2008 Core Institute study: http://www.core.siuc.edu/pdfs/report08.pdf. Based out of the University of Southern Illinois, the Core

Institute is the largest statistical database for alcohol and other drug use among college-aged students.

3. Ibid.

4. Leviticus 23:4–44.

5. Mark 2:13–17; John 12:1–10.

6. John 2:1–12.

7. Matthew 22:1–14; 25:1–13; Luke 12:35–40; 14:15–23.

8. Will Willimon and Tom Naylor make this case in *The Abandoned Generation*, as does Tom Wolfe in his devastating 2004 novel *I Am Charlotte Simmons*.

9. One homeless man told me a story about a group of teens on a motorcycle who hit him in the face with a paper plate full of human feces, covered in whipped cream.

10. Psalm 98:7–9.

Chapter 11: Sex

1. A Kaiser Study found fewer than half of all high school students reported having had sexual intercourse, declining from 53 percent in 1995 to 47 percent in 2005. (Kaiser Family Foundations, Sexual Health Statistics for Teenagers and Young Adults in the United States. [September 2006]). This statistic is *down*, that's right I said down, 10 percent from just ten years earlier.

2. Ibid.

3. One college student I spoke with made this comment and I think it reflects a lot of people's experience. If you're not having intercourse you are strange. Maybe they'll even make a movie about you if you retain your virginity into your forties.

4. Richard Walzer, *Galen on Christians and Jews* (New York: Oxford, 1947).

5. Lauren Winner, *Real Sex* (Grand Rapids: Brazos, 2005), 123. I love this definition and it is the one I'm working from in this chapter.

6. Two movies released recently have story lines where friends agree to sleep together and then try to keep the relationship strictly physical. But the thing is, in both cases, they can't do it. The drama in these movies comes from the fact that even though we know sex is more than just intercourse, we keep trying to act like it's not.

7. Genesis 1:27–31; 2:7–25.

8. Genesis 3:8.

9. Genesis 3:10–11.

10. Genesis 3:11–13.

11. Genesis 3:23–24.

12. See pages 40–41 in Rob Bell's *Sex God* (Grand Rapids: Zondervan, 2007). I owe this whole paragraph to him. The book is really excellent and a great read if you want to dive deeper into the connections between sexuality and spirituality.

13. Pun totally intended.

14. I know, I know, it's a Marvin Gaye song, but it fits our context does it not? Pun intended here as well.

15. See chapter 3, "Communal Sex," in *Real Sex*. Lauren Winner's book is as good as it gets for fresh and helpful perspectives on good sex in our day. I cannot recommend it highly enough.

16. Current statistics are that one in four women will be sexually assaulted, and one in five men. Check out this stat sheet from the Crimes Against Children Research Center: http://www.unh.edu/ccrc/sexual-abuse/factsheet_assault.html for more information.

17. Consider the way American sexual appetites and opinions affect the global pornography market and sexual trafficking. Every time you click on certain websites or buy certain media, you put money into a system that enslaves and dehumanizes thousands of women and children a year. This is one of the things that makes God angry, as it should make us angry too. Go to http://www.notforsalecampaign.org/ and find out how you can be part of the solution.

18. No pun intended here.

19. C. S. Lewis, *Mere Christianity* (New York: Harper Collins, 2001), 95.

Chapter 12: Go in Peace

1. Paul made this same point in 1 Corinthians 15. While arguing that Jesus' resurrection is the turning point of human history and following in Him means becoming re-humanized, Paul rounds on some folks who are denying this to be the case. These church members are saying that the resurrection never happened and as a result, people should just do whatever they desire. Because there is no renewal of all things, they said, people should grab all the sex, money, and power that they can in the time they have on earth. This was highly influential on the new Christians (as you might imagine), but not because it was being taught directly—the influence came from the lived lives of the community members themselves. This is why Paul closed out his argument by quoting the Greek poet Meander, saying, "But don't be so naïve—there's another saying you know well—Bad company corrupts good habits" (1 Cor. 15:33). You are indeed who you hang out with.

2. I found this quote attributed to everyone from Oscar Wilde, to Mark Twain, to Groucho Marx. Good luck sourcing it.

3. This phrase is used to describe Tyler Durden in Chuck Palahniuk's *Fight Club*. I've always found it a fitting description for someone doing faith well in our day.

4. Matthew 7:3.

Wisdom for the Road

1. You can read the transcript, but I recommend the video version. Both available here: http://www.dartmouth.edu/~commence/speeches/2011/obrien-speech.html.

ACKNOWLEDGMENTS

I could never have written a book like this on my own. This project has been a collaborative effort from day one, so if you will please indulge me I'd like to say "Thank you" to a few folks:

First, I have to say thanks to Don. Without your dream, talent, and vision, this project would have never gotten off the ground. Likewise, thanks to Frank and Lindsey for bringing me on board and trusting me to run with it.

Thanks to Dane Anthony for sharing your years of wisdom about how teens transition best into college life (Dane's website, www.collegeparent101.com, is a great resource) and to Micah Weedman for the countless conversations about what goes wrong after they do.

Thanks to Julia Carruthers-Thorne for your selfless help in reading, proofing, and commenting on nearly all the initial chapters (even the ones that didn't make the book.)

Thanks to Steve Levebre and Sally Chambers for being such faithful and helpful readers when the going got tough.

Also, thanks to Molly, Justin, Matt, Annie, and everyone else who helped brainstorm ideas and shared their stories. I also want to thank Jerry and my faith community at St. Bartholomew's. I am so grateful I get to follow Jesus with you all and consider it a gift to be part of our community.

A big thanks to Alee Anderson for your collaboration on so much of the content, form, and structure of this project. You brought out the strength in my voice as a writer and made me sound better than I would have sounded on my own. Also, thanks to Ashley Linne for keeping us both moving the right direction.

Finally, thanks to my wonderful wife Kristin. The sacrifices you made and encouragements you offered made the difference. Thanks for loving me the way you do and believing in me when I did not believe in myself. I love you more than I can say.